APR '98

Beyond Tokenism

PARENTS AS PARTNERS IN LITERACY

Beyond Tokenism

PARENTS AS PARTNERS IN LITERACY

Trevor H. Cairney
Lynne Munsie

HEINEMANN
Portsmouth, NH

Heinemann
A division of Reed Elsevier Inc.
361 Hanover Street
Portsmouth, NH 03801-3912

Offices and agents throughout the world

Copyright © 1995 Trevor Cairney and Lynne Munsie

First Published 1992 by
Australian Reading Association
187 Lygon Street
Carlton, Victoria 3053
Australia

Library of Congress Cataloging-in-Publication Data
Cairney, Trevor.
        Beyond tokenism : parents as partners in literacy / Trevor H. Cairney and Lynne Munsie.
          p. cm.
        "First published 1992 by Australian Reading Association"—T.p. verso
        Includes bibliographical references and index.
        ISBN 0-435-08832-7
          1. Education—Parent participation. 2. Literacy. 3. Home and school.
        4. Education—Parent participation—Australia—New South Wales—Case studies.
        I. Munsie, Lynne. II. Title.
        LC225.C29 1995
        370.19'31—dc20   94-31882
                                                                                      CIP

Printed in the United States of America on acid-free paper
99 98 97 96 95   1 2 3 4 5 6 7 8 9

Contents

Foreword

This book is the culmination of two years' work with families and schools in Western Sydney and Newcastle. It began at Lethbridge Park Primary and Lethbridge Park Preschool in 1990, and was later extended to Stockton Primary and Stockton Preschool. The stimulus for the initial work came from a grant from the NSW Ministry of Education and Youth Affairs. A committee consisting of teachers and parents was formed to prepare a proposal. The proposal was submitted and funding provided for the parent literacy project which has become known as TTALL (Talk To a Literacy Learner). The TTALL project and its outcomes provided the starting point for this book. It provided us with the opportunity to focus our attention on the issue of parental involvement in literacy learning, and to make the connections that have led ultimately to this book.

It has been TTALL that convinced us of the need for this book. Our experiences in that program highlighted a number of significant issues. First, that parents are one of the most vital elements in any child's education. Second, that the quantity and quality of the literacy transactions in which parents and children engage are vital for any child's growth as a literacy learner. Third, that many parents hold numerous faulty assumptions about their role as supporters of their children's literacy. Fourth, that schools reinforce many of these assumptions by failing to involve parents as equal partners in their children's education. Fifth, that many attempts to involve parents in their children's literacy education are tokenistic and at times patronising.

In the chapters that follow we attempt to answer a number of questions:

- Why should we involve parents?
- How should we involve parents?
- In what ways can we involve parents?
- What are our responsibilities towards parents?

As we answer these questions it is our aim to dispel a number of beliefs and assumptions held by teachers and schools concerning:

- what parents can and cannot do;
- what parents desire for their children;
- how parent involvement should be designed and implemented;
- the role that parents can and should play in their children's literacy development.

We trust that the ideas which we share will be of use to you as teachers or parents. We look forward to the conversations that will follow as readers respond to this book. We are already grateful for the many conversations that have allowed this book to be written.

We are particularly appreciative of the insights of parents at Lethbridge Park Preschool and Primary School and Stockton Preschool and Primary School. The conversations that we have had with these parents have pushed us to re-examine our own assumptions about the role that parents play in literacy learning.

The writing of this book has been a privilege for both of us. We trust that it will remind readers of, and awaken them to, the vital role that parents play as partners in literacy learning.

Literacy and the home

Parents have an important part to play in the education of their children.

That statement is a fairly reasonable beginning to any paper or book on parents and literacy. Or is it? Behind it could be any number of assumptions and views on parents' roles in children's educational development. There seem to be many conceptualisations of the parents' role in schooling. Some see parents as 'keepers' who ensure that children are well fed, loved, and groomed and sent to school to be adequately 'trained' each day. Others see parents as home-based 'warders' ensuring that standards of behaviour are conformed to, good habits set, and school related tasks completed. Another view seems to be that parents are meant to be compliant 'apprentices' working with children at school (as helpers) and at home on a range of simple, but effective, training tasks.

All of these views have several things in common. First, they assume that parents have only a limited responsibility in relation to their children as learners. Second, they assume that the school is the site of the 'main game'. Third, they offer parents only a token role in children's education.

At the outset, we wish to reject all views of parent involvement which fail to recognise the integral role that parents play in their children's education. Parents are not simply a minor part of the educational process, some variable to be considered and addressed. Learning is a social process which has its beginnings in parent/child relationships which are based on shared meaning. The home provides both the beginning and foundation for learning.

Our book is concerned with the building of partnerships with parents in their children's education. Specifically, our focus is on literacy. Our interest in literacy is both a personal interest and a recognition of its centrality in the learning processes of all children. In the chapters that follow we explore the importance of parents in the literacy development of children, and examine ways to involve parents as partners in this learning.

PARENTS' ROLES AS CHILDREN'S FIRST LANGUAGE 'TEACHERS'

Teachers, educators and researchers have long pointed to the almost miraculous way in which children master the complexities of spoken language before the age of five years. Parents play a dominant role in this development, intuitively prompting and prodding their children towards meaning making. From birth parents treat their babies as if they are communicating with them, and they respond to them in the light of this purpose (Wells, 1986).

The child focuses on meaning and the caregiver responds to the meanings he or she makes. In the context of this purposeful exchange, meanings develop. In this way, language develops as the child actively participates in communicative acts, and engages in a constructive process of meaning making (Lindfors, 1985).

The parent's role in this is as a listener, prompter, information giver, asker of questions, but all the time a fellow meaning maker interested in the communication process (Cairney, 1989b; 1990). It seems that the keys to early language development are the volume of opportunities to make meaning (Wells, 1983), the degree of one-to-one interaction with adults where the adult is talking about matters that are of interest and concern to the child (Wells, 1986), and finally, the type and nature of adult interaction with children (Snow, 1983).

But ironically, our interest in the role parents play in literacy development has been stimulated by the observation of a surprising anomaly. We have frequently observed that many of the same parents who fulfilled the rich and complex role in spoken language development described above suddenly begin to fulfil more limited roles in the literacy learning of their children once school age is reached. The same parents who responded to their pre-school children as meaning makers suddenly begin to focus on spelling, punctuation, sounding out words, syllabification, and so on. Shared meaning is no longer the major focus.

LITERACY'S ROOTS IN CULTURE

The anomaly that we have just described reflects a cultural view of school literacy that requires parents to fulfil the role of corrector, driller, and interrogator of text. Such views of the parent's role, as the child encounters school literacy, reflect culture. But not only are parental roles culturally determined, the way literacy is viewed reflects culture. In fact, it has been argued by some that the extent to which children cope with schooling is related closely to a range of cultural factors (Heath, 1983).

This connection with culture has been illustrated by Heath's (1983) well-known ethnography in three communities in the Piedmont Carolinas. Heath found considerable cultural variation in the acquisition of oral language, and the manner in which parents introduced children to literacy. By focusing closely on story reading she was able to document significant differences in community styles of literacy socialisation.

Children in a white middle-class community (Maintown) were socialised into a life in which books and information gained from them were seen as having a significant role in learning. They interacted with children for 6 months in book reading events, asking information questions, relating the content to life situations and encouraging them to tell their own narratives. In a white working-class community (Roadville) children were also involved in book reading, but this centred on alphabet and number books, real-life stories, nursery rhymes and bible stories. The focus for these parents was usually on factual recounts of events. Parents asked factual questions about the books, but did not attempt to relate the books to the children's lives.

Finally, the parents within a poor black community (Trackton) rarely provided book reading events. As well, the questions these parents asked were different. They did not ask their children to name or describe the features of their world. As well, they used oral stories of a different kind, focusing mainly on fictional stories or familiar events in new contexts.

Clearly, each of these communities was inadvertently preparing its children in different ways for schooling. Heath found that children in Maintown performed well in school. Roadville children on the other hand did well in the early grades, but had difficulty after grade three when a greater emphasis was placed on analytic, predictive and evaluative questioning, which required them to think more abstractly and independently. However, Trackton children were unsuccessful in school right from the early grades.

What was happening in each of these communities was that the place literacy enjoyed in their culture was helping to prepare these children, to greater and lesser extents, to succeed or fail in the school system.

Consistently, research has found that school factors (e.g. resources, class size, classroom organisation and methods) are relatively minor factors in student achievement at school (Hanushek, 1981; Jencks et al., 1972; Thompson, 1985). Differences in family backgrounds have a far more significant impact on student achievement. Some have gone as far as to suggest that the cumulative effect of a range of family-related factors probably accounts for the greatest proportion of variability in student literacy performance (Rutter, Tizzard & Witmore, 1970; Thompson, 1985).

The reality is that schools staffed by middle-class teachers reflect middle-class, culturally defined views of what literacy is and how it is best developed. It takes little effort to determine why specific cultural groups experience difficulties coping with literacy in such a context. As Bourdieu (1977) has pointed out, schools inconsistently tap the social and cultural resources of society, privileging specific groups by emphasising particular linguistic styles, curricula and authority patterns.

One way in which these basic cultural influences can be minimised is by involving parents more closely in school education. The purpose in breaking down the barriers between home and school is not to coerce, or even persuade, parents to take on the literacy definitions held by teachers. Rather, it is to enable both teachers and parents to understand the way each defines, values and uses literacy as part of cultural practices. In this way schooling can be adjusted to meet the needs of families. Parents in turn can also be given the opportunity to observe and understand the definitions of literacy that schools support, and which ultimately empower individuals to take their place in society.

PARENT PARTICIPATION

Attempts to bring schools and communities closer together have taken many forms, and at times have been anything but helpful. Bruner (1980, in Briggs & Potter, 1990) has pointed out that parent involvement in schooling is often a 'dustbin term' which can mean all things to all men. Potter (in Briggs & Potter, 1990) also points out that parent involvement programs are often 'shallow, ineffectual, confusing, and frustrating to both parents and teachers'.

One of the reasons for the failure of some programs is that many teachers have negative attitudes about parents and parent involvement. These teachers sometimes claim that parents are apathetic, and come to school only to criticise (Briggs & Potter, 1990). These teacher attitudes appear to be particularly evident when the parents are from lower socio-economic groups.

Others have suggested that the failure of some programs to attract parental interest may be due to parents not feeling competent to deal with school work. As well, it has been argued that this phenomenon may reflect the fact that these parents feel insecure in the school setting, and fearful about participation in the learning of their children (Moles, 1982; Greenberg, 1989).

As Mavrogenes (1990) points out, teachers and principals may need to question the assumption that low-income parents do not care about their children's education. It is likely that most parents are willing to help with their children's education, but many may have little idea concerning how to provide this help.

Halsey and Midwinter (1972, in Briggs & Potter, 1990) have argued that the best way to overcome some of these problems and to empower working-class students is to change the nature of education so that students will be equipped with the knowledge and skills necessary to gain power over their own community. This, they argued, requires the transformation of primary schools into focal points for their communities, thus bringing teachers and parents closer together, and leading subsequently to changed attitudes on the part of both parties. Such schools, it is argued, should aim to develop self-esteem and provide students with power over their lives.

Unfortunately, some schools have adopted a very narrow definition of parent involvement, which primarily seeks to determine what parents can do for teachers, rather than what schools can do for families. This view is often evidenced by parents filling a variety of unpaid teacher aide or custodial roles.

Parents must be viewed as equal partners. There must be a reciprocal relationship. We need to go beyond involvement and recognise the vital role that parents play in education. As Kruger and Mahon (1990) point out, 'parental involvement in literacy learning has much greater value than as an add-on to what teachers do' (p. 4).

If parents are to be viewed as partners in children's learning then teachers need to re-examine their assumptions about parents.

SIX MYTHS THAT IMPEDE PARENT INVOLVEMENT

We believe that the starting point for parent participation programs that move beyond tokenism is to dispel the myths that limit options for parent involvement. Each of these myths needs to be challenged.

MYTH 1 PARENTS ARE NOT INTERESTED IN THEIR CHILDREN'S EDUCATION

Our work has shown that virtually all parents are vitally interested in their children's education. Of course, the way parents show this interest varies greatly. Not all parents check homework, set work schedules, obtain resources for assignment work, or attend school regularly seeking advice.

Thompson (1992) found that while homework was important to a child's achievement at school, at least three major models of homework were held by different parent groups, each characterised by specific practices. These parental practices are culturally defined. The result of these varying cultural practices is that mismatches between parent and teacher expectations of the home's role frequently occur. The lack of definitions of educational support consistent with the teacher's cannot simply be interpreted as a lack of parental concern. While parents involve themselves in schooling to differing extents, with some rarely appearing at school, all parents desire to see their children educated.

MYTH 2   ONLY SOME PARENTS ARE INTERESTED IN THEIR CHILDREN

This myth often has a cultural basis. Some teachers frequently assume that specific groups such as the poorly educated, specific ethnic minorities and single parents are less interested in their children's education than the white middle class. This myth is often evident in a variety of comments. For example:

> You'll never get the parents interested here. They couldn't care less. They never come near the school, you're wasting your time trying to involve them. Only the better parents ever turn up.

Our work has shown that most, if not all, parents are interested. If parents see that activities associated with schooling have relevance to their children's growth as learners they will be involved. Smrekar (1992) argues that parents will show little interest in school events or activities unless their children are involved in these events or activities. Meetings, committees or formal functions are unlikely to gain support. She argues that this is an inevitable consequence of the pressures of twentieth-century living, not parental disinterest.

MYTH 3   MIDDLE-CLASS PARENTS ARE BETTER PARENTS

Such a myth would hardly deserve comment were it not for the fact that it is widely held. Because schools invariably invoke particular curricula, linguistic styles and so on (Bourdieu, 1977), teachers tend to assume that parents who hold beliefs about schooling similar to their own are 'better' parents. However, our work has shown that while parents hold different definitions of literacy and how it is developed, qualitative judgements concerning their value as parents are not justified. Lareau (1989) also argues strongly that higher social classes do not possess greater interest in their children's schooling. Rather, they possess greater resources to intervene in schooling and to provide their children with support. These resources include education, income, occupational status, style of work and social network.

MYTH 4 IT IS DIFFICULT TO GET PARENTS INVOLVED

This myth is closely linked with Myth 1. There is little doubt that it is difficult to involve parents in some school-related activities. For example, parents are often not interested in parents and citizens organisations, parent–teacher nights, speech nights and so on. This phenomenon is hardly surprising. The average parents and citizens meeting is of little interest even for the most ardent lover of formal meetings. While this does not have to be the case, it is a reality in many schools. Schools and teachers need to consider the type of activities initiated for parents.

MYTH 5 YOU ONLY GET THE PARENTS YOU DON'T NEED TO SEE

Some teachers are reluctant to pursue initiatives because of the belief that the parents who involve themselves are those who need less support than those who do not become involved. This is another myth that is culturally laden. It is underpinned by at least one faulty assumption. That is, that there are some parents who know how to cope with school, and some who do not; some whose views on schooling align with those of the school, and some whose views do not. Such an assumption fails to understand that parents are partners in education, and that schools must be responsive to, and informed by, the needs of all parents and children. Even those parents not seen to conform to teacher expectations must be listened to and involved.

Such an assumption also assumes that the problem with non-involvement in school activities rests with the parents. Inherent within this is a failure to accept responsibility for all that is done by the school to involve parents. It should hardly be surprising that some parents find some activities in which they can be involved at school useful, while others do not. The challenge is to find a variety of ways to bring parents and schools closer together. This is the topic of much of what follows in this book.

MYTH 6 PARENTS ARE NOT CAPABLE OF HELPING THEIR CHILDREN TO LEARN

This myth is once again based on a flawed assumption. That is, parents have little to offer beyond the menial in the education of their children. Our experience with the TTALL project has shown us that parents know far more about language and learning than most teachers realise. What needs to be remembered is that parents were in fact their children's first 'teachers' and were largely responsible for introducing their children to the complexities of oral language. Furthermore, most are engaged in the literacy practices which are the very goals of our educational system. The majority of parents are readers and writers in the 'real' world. As such they have an insider's view on literacy practices, and yet so often they feel alienated from much of what is done in the name of literacy in our schools. It seems that the ability of parents to support their children is often impeded by the 'schooling' of literacy. A starting point to overcome this problem is to transform school practices so that they are more culturally relevant to the communities for which they were created.

CHALLENGING THE MYTHS

In the chapters that follow it is our intention to challenge these myths and to provide strategies for implementing programs that move beyond them to establish genuine partnerships in education. We believe that parents have a critical role in their children's educational development. It is our intention to explore how schools might set about ensuring that parents are involved as partners in literacy education.

In Chapter 2 we review the complete range of possibilities for home/school links, and consider the key influences that shape our various parent initiatives.

2

Rethinking parent involvement programs

As outlined in Chapter 1, schools almost universally accept that parents need to have some role in their children's education during the years of schooling. What is in question, however, is the form that this involvement takes. The way schools have traditionally attempted to involve parents has been through a range of support initiatives.

Petit (1980) has outlined a model describing levels of parent participation that is of some help in understanding what form parent participation has taken. He suggests that the first level is monitoring and is essentially teacher initiated. It takes the form of letters, informal talks, class meetings and other forms of communication.

The second level is informing, and involves the provision of more detailed information about school policies, organisational procedures, aims, expectations and the like. This is usually achieved through notices, direct reporting, parent–teacher conferences, home visits by teachers and well produced written materials.

The third level is that of participation and essentially includes some type of involvement in the activities of the classroom or school. The examples Petit provides are varied but include schools where parents help to produce materials, and another where the school ran a series of parent in-service workshops on reading.

We find Petit's classification system helpful, but for us it does not go quite far enough. While it describes three broad categories of involvement it does not provide for the considerable diversity within these categories which we have observed. 'Participation', for example, covers a myriad models.

Rather than trying simply to categorise parent involvement, we have found it useful to assess any parent initiative in relation to a number of key variables. There appear to be four main variables which influence the nature and conduct of any program:

- CONTENT — What information is shared?
- PROCESS — How is information shared?
- SOURCE — Who has initiated the involvement?
- CONTROL — Who is in control of the program?

CONTENT OF PARENT PROGRAMS

As the diagram below indicates, at its most basic level the content of parent initiatives is little more than information about school activities and procedures. On the other hand, some programs offer substantial programs that involve parents in their children's education. What is worth noting is that at each level there are different opportunities for two-way communication between parents and teachers. At the more general school level, the advice given is not very specific to individual student needs. However, as we move further towards full participation, parent and student needs are catered for at an individual level. We will describe briefly each of these sub-types.

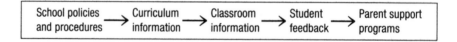

SCHOOL POLICIES AND PROCEDURES

The provision of information about school policies and procedures is obviously an important function. In some schools all new students are given a booklet which contains general information about school services, routines and policies. At times this type of resource will contain:

- information on reading schemes;
- home reading guides;
- library borrowing details;
- guidelines concerning children's independent reading.

As well, leaflets are often distributed which contain advice for parents about reading to and with their children. In some cases these are developed by schools, whereas in other cases material developed at the school systems level is used (see opposite).

LETHBRIDGE PARK PUBLIC SCHOOL

Dear Parents,

We would like to share some positive ways you could help your child in reading development. The Read With Me Club provides encouragement and incentives for your child.

Set aside a regular time each night to read to your child. The bedtime story is the most valuable way to ensure a healthy attitude towards reading.

Make this time enjoyable and free from tension.

Your child may bring home a book for you to share together. Listen to your child read. If he or she is at the beginning stages of reading, help him or her to point to the words. Do not isolate letters and sounds. Reading is gaining meaning, not just saying words. Encourage your child to gain sense from the story. Resist jumping in and correcting errors but ask questions like "Does this make sense? What does it start with?"

Our aim is to create in children a love of books and to lead them towards being independent readers. To do this, we teach them strategies to cope with an unknown word. These strategies appear on a chart labelled "What To Do When You Come to a Word You Don't Know."

This chart is on the back of the child's Read With Me Club folder. You can become familiar with this so that you will understand just what your child is attempting to do.

Encourage your child to retell a story in his or her own words.

Words are everywhere. When you go shopping, or on outings, read signs and labels.

When your child reaches a target - 25, 50, 75 etc. he/she will be given a reward to encourage him/her to keep going.

E.R. HEMMENS   A. McLELLAN
PRINCIPAL   DEPUTY PRINCIPAL

While material of this type is clearly of use, it has, at best, only minimal impact on parents as supporters of literacy learning.

CURRICULUM INFORMATION

With an ever-changing curriculum, schools need to provide parents with information concerning the various curricula that are followed. This is provided infrequently. It is often given as part of parents and citizens meetings, or as part of parent–teacher nights. Topics vary greatly, but might include:
- What is the place of spelling in the 'new' English curriculum?
- Is grammar important?
- What is the role of literature in the curriculum?

One of the weaknesses of this type of activity is that it places teachers in the role of expert and the parent as recipient of their wisdom. Not surprisingly, those parents who were glad to escape school when younger, to avoid teachers, are reluctant to attend such activities.

Another problem is that the 'workshops' are often lectures that do little to equip parents to support their children as learners.

CLASSROOM INFORMATION

While there is a place for school-level information sessions on curricular issues there is also a need for more specific classroom-based information. Many teachers provide specific information on their literacy programs. This frequently includes the following information:
- information on research work (see the example opposite);
- classroom policies on spelling, writing, reading;
- home editing checklists;
- reading guides, including space for parent signatures and records of reading;
- newsletters containing descriptions of current work, helpful hints, handwriting style guides, etc.

Information of this type is clearly of greater practical value to parents. In our experience it also tends to reduce the chances of literacy programs being misunderstood. Nevertheless, this type of information sharing provides little opportunity for the teacher to learn more about parents. Nor is there any guarantee that the advice is acted upon.

STUDENT FEEDBACK

All schools provide some type of feedback concerning student literacy progress. At the very least, reports are given twice per year. While these reports

Project - Hot air balloons.

Research the topic. Find out who invented the hot air balloon. What were hot air balloons used for in the past? What uses do they have these days? What makes hot air balloons work?

Due date: Wednesday, July 1, 1992.

"How do I do a project?" - I hear this often.
Well, I'm going to tell you:
- Use either cardboard or a project book;
- Have a clear heading;
- Answer the questions — extra information will get
                extra marks; underline headings.
- Use colours - but make sure it does not look messy;
- If you use pictures, diagrams or charts make sure they are clearly labelled — and they sometimes look better if they are drawn around — for example 🖼 or 🖼 ; (but more neatly!).
- get your project in on time — it is not fair if some children get more time than others (except in sickness)
- write clearly and neatly — get someone to check your rough copy before you to your finished copy.

Parents: I have had information available in class for the children to access for the past week-and-a-half, so if they say they do not have any information, please tell them to see me.

Thanks,
Merryn Gittins

typically contain little information, they offer some indication on relative performance in literacy.

In more recent times some teachers have begun to use portfolio assessment procedures and 'focused evaluation' in literacy which offer far more detailed and useful information on student progress. A typical portfolio might contain:

- samples of work, e.g. first and final drafts of several representative pieces of writing;
- a list of books read in a specific period of time;
- children's self-evaluations of their progress.

'Focused evaluation' is used by some schools as a replacement for traditional reports. It involves teachers systematically evaluating the progress of a sub-group of students each week (see opposite). In this way all parents receive an evaluation every 4–6 weeks. The evaluation includes a summary of observations made for the period and an opportunity for parents to respond.

Of even greater use are direct contact meetings between parents and teachers to discuss student progress and to hear about class activities. This type of activity provides an opportunity for two-way communication between parents and teachers. Such parent–teacher sessions can occur during the day or evening and typically include:

- an overview of the teacher's classroom organisation, program, methods;
- the teacher's personal philosophy on education;
- details on assessment;
- a description of specific ideas for involving parents in literacy;
- time for questions and answers;
- specific consultation times for discussions concerning student progress.

This type of activity has the potential to allow teachers and parents to learn from each other. However, there are problems. First, many teachers claim that only some parents attend such functions (e.g. mothers, and parents of high achievers). Second, most activities of this type provide only limited opportunity for parents to share their needs, ideas and so on. Third, they occur infrequently, therefore reducing opportunities for significant parent learning. Fourth, parents are not always clear about the possibilities of these meetings and how they might gain practical assistance from them.

PARENT SUPPORT PROGRAMS

This final category is concerned with those initiatives that have as their focus the provision of opportunities for parents to learn about literacy, and about the ways they can support their children as literacy learners. The form that such participation programs take can vary greatly. The common forms include:

- parents as helpers, e.g. reading to children, listening to children read, helping with spelling programs;

LETHBRIDGE PARK P.S.

Dear Parents,

During this year _____ are going to trial a different approach to reporting on your child's progress. Each week, six children will be observed and notes taken about the learning that is taking place during activities. A summary of these observations will be sent home at the end of the week, outlining areas of your child's growth during this period of time.

This method means that each family will receive a report at least twice a term. It will also enable you to have greater input into your child's education.

Instead of the half yearly and end of year reports, of old, you will receive a summary of the focused evaluation carried out on your child's progress over that period of time.

An essential part of the programme will be the communication that is set in motion between teacher/child, teacher/parent and parent/child.

Feel free to contact me if you have any queries.

- parents as aides, e.g. typing students' stories, assisting in the library;
- educational programs designed to help parents support their children.

While all of these sub-types have the advantage that they actually get

Lethbridge Park P.S.

Copeland Road
Lethbridge Park
2770

NAME: _Tennille_

CLASS: _1/2M_   TERM: _2_   WEEK: _6_

Tennille has settled into her new class quite well. She is a very keen motivated learner who is always trying to please. In writing, she writes well with alot of invented spelling and also alot of known spelling words. In reading, she reads fluently with quite a good comprehension. She does related reading activities very well. In maths we did take aways from 10 which Tennille did very well and she attempted from 20 with concrete material. We've started multiplication with making groups and pictorial eg's and she understands this process. We've also done time activities and volume activities with sand/water and containers in groups which Tennille benefited from - sharing ideas and listening to others and coming up with recorded results. Good work.

PRINCIPAL: _____

TEACHER: _RMorris_

Parent Comments.

When I read this report, I was very pleased with tennilles work. She has always been very keen to please.

I believe tennille has a lot of ability and will do well with incouragement both from home and school. The most important thing I tell tennille is as long as she is trying her best. It doesn't matter if she comes home with a poor report or a good report. The most important thing is that she is trying the best she can. TENNILLE s mind is always clicking and she gets bored quickly when she can't express herself. I am pleased tennille can express herself in your class as her attitude to school has changed. She now enjoys it and is keen to learn. Your comments have showed she is coming up with very Good Results

EXCELLENT WORK   Mrs Morris

parents into schools, in our experience the last described has the potential to lead to the greatest long-term changes in the parents' ability to support their children. It is this type of program that is the major focus of this book and which will be described in greater detail in following chapters.

PARENT HELPERS

Parents are very important to Lethbridge Park school. There are many local parents who help in classrooms, the library or who take home books to cover in plastic etc. We would like to make an open invitation to all kindergarten parents to join us at school from the first day. If you would like to remain at school with your child for some of the day, you are welcome to do so. We would ask that you take part in the activities which the teacher has organised, working with several children, not just your own. In this way you will be able to see what your child is doing at school and be a part of his/her new life.

We hope the above has answered some of your questions about the school, we are sure you will have many more - that gives you the excuse to come and get to know us! A more detailed booklet of information will be sent home when your child starts school next year.

Thank you for your attendance today.

E.R. HEMMENS   A. McLELLAN
PRINCIPAL   DEPUTY PRINCIPAL

PROCESSES USED IN PARENT PROGRAMS

The processes used as part of parent involvement are also critical factors in the determination of the nature and, we argue, the effectiveness of home/school initiatives.

It is important also to consider both the communication processes and the learning processes used as part of common home/school initiatives.

COMMUNICATION PROCESSES

There appear to be three broad communication strategies used. The first is what we would label ONE-WAY COMMUNICATION. This is primarily the dissemination of information from the school to parents. Letters, policy documents, lectures on specific topics and so on, are all examples of this type of communication.

The second we have labelled INFORMATION SHARING. This is still predominantly the sharing of information by the school, but does provide an opportunity for parents to express their views on a variety of issues. Examples of this type of communication process are workshops on set topics, parent–teacher nights, and surveys of parent needs and attitudes. In each of these examples, there is still only limited communication between parents and the school.

In each of the two above processes of communication the assumption is primarily that parents need to receive information. The third category of communication processes is based on the assumption that each partner in the educational process has something to share, and something to learn. In one sense, this is the only category in which 'real' communication takes place. We refer to it as IDEA EXCHANGE. What is different about this type of communicative process is that it is designed to permit all parties to share ideas and grow in understanding. Examples include parent participation projects that involve parents working with children in the school, community based workshops, and programs like the TTALL program, which is described in Chapter 6.

TEACHING/LEARNING PROCESSES

The processes used for teaching and learning are closely aligned with the above communication processes. It seems that the teaching/learning processes used in home/school programs have varied along a continuum from INFORMATION TRANSFER to INTERACTIVE LEARNING. The former is characterised by the sharing of information in such forms as written information, lectures and films from one party (typically teachers) to the other (typically parents). In its most extreme form, little opportunity is provided for the sharing of ideas and reflection on and discussion of the ideas that are outlined.

Interactive learning, in its most extreme form, involves an integrated cycle of input, demonstration, discussion, trialling, and reflection. Such a model of teaching and learning was the basis of the TTALL program and is represented diagrammatically below.

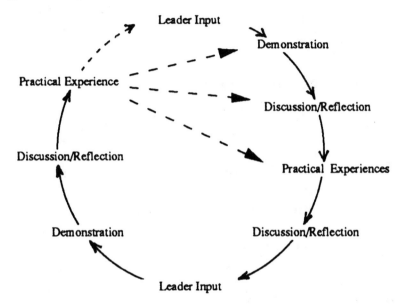

Between each of these extremes many variations have been evident, each of which is related to the content to be shared and the purpose of the home/school initiative. For example, there is a place for the sharing of basic school procedures and information on community resources. In such cases, a process of simple information transfer is probably justifiable. There are also times when parents do want information on school curriculum initiatives (such as a new mathematics program). In such cases a simple 'one off' workshop may be sufficient.

In terms of processes, schools need to make use of all communication and learning possibilities. What needs always to be kept in mind are the strengths and limitations of the processes used. For example, schools should not expect significant growth in parental knowledge of literacy and in their roles as supporters of their children's learning, through a newsletter or the occasional workshop.

SOURCE OF THE HOME/SCHOOL INITIATIVES

Another important criterion that has had an impact on the shape of any home/ school activity is the source of the initiative. In our experience, almost all such activities are initiated by the school. Rarely are activities run which have been solely initiated by parents.

It should be our aim as educators to create environments in which parents feel they can initiate suggestions, and in which these are frequently acted upon. It is our belief that the most significant changes occur when parents take the initiative.

CONTROL OF HOME/SCHOOL INITIATIVES

The final criterion which has influenced the shape and nature of home/school initiatives is control. This criterion is related closely to all of the previous criteria. Learning theorists have long argued that effective learning requires individuals to be able to take control. There is little control in the hands of parents for the majority of home/school initiatives. As a result, there is frequently minimal parent involvement and commitment.

It should be obvious that if a school provides a participation program that reflects parent needs, and which uses INTERACTIVE LEARNING leading to genuine IDEA EXCHANGE, parents will be in control of their own learning. It is our contention that when these conditions are met significant benefits are derived for schools and parents.

USING THE FULL RANGE OF HOME/SCHOOL INITIATIVES

The above discussion has shown that there are many ways in which home/ school initiatives have been established. While much of this book is devoted to outlining in detail programs that have stressed interactive learning, parent/ school partnership and idea exchange, we see a place for the full range of home/ school initiatives. The following grid is provided to indicate the full range of initiatives that are possible. It is based on all of the above criteria, but is shaped by issues of content and process. Control and source are closely integrated with these two key criteria.

As the grid opposite shows there are many ways in which home/school initiatives have been established. Nevertheless, in our experience many

Home/School Literacy Initiatives

	PROCESS		
CONTENT	**Written Communication**	**Workshops/Meetings**	**Participation Programmes**
School Policies & Procedures	• School information booklets for new enrollees • School suggestions concerning home reading	• Discussion of school policies at P & C meetings • Description of school procedures at parent information nights	Involvement of parents in policy formulations: - discipline - library procedures - parent involvement
Curriculum Information	• School policies on spelling, grammar etc • Description of schemes adopted for reading • Information sheets on new curricula • Extracts from curriculum documents	• Workshops on 'Process Writing' • Demonstration of Paired Reading • Workshop on editing children's writing	Involvement of parents in: - literacy Inservice initiatives - school curriculum planning
Classroom Information	• Description of procedures for homework • Home reading guide • Editing checklists • Ideas for research writing	• Parent/Teacher meetings on: - Reading methods - Place of spelling in classroom - Class writing publication programming • Parent workshop on research writing.	• Parents as reading partners • Parent involvement in writing conferences • Parents as resource people sharing insights about their use of literacy
Student Feedback	• School reports • Portfolios of work • Classroom publications • Class and school newsletters.	• Parent/Teacher discussions • Parent interviews • Parent meeting on school reporting procedures	• Observation of children in classrooms • Parents as reading partners • Parent involvement in writing conferences • Parent assistance with research work
Parental Support of their Children	• Parent leaflets on literacy - How to read to your child - Responding to your child's writing - What about grammar • Information on listening and talking to your child	• Workshops on: - reading to your child - listening to your child - responding to your child's writing - using the library - computer literacy • Visiting experts on issues of relevance (P & C and Parent/Teacher meetings)	• Workshops on using "paired reading" • Observation of skilled use of writing conferences • Structured parent involvement programmes (eg. TTALL)

schools use only a limited range of these initiatives, primarily at the SCHOOL PROCEDURES and WRITTEN COMMUNICATION end of the content and process continua. We would encourage schools to use the grid above as a starting point in the evaluation of current school practices. As stated previously, it is the aim of this book to encourage schools to consider the full range of initiatives at their disposal.

3

Towards a model for complete parent participation

In the previous chapter we looked at the various forms that home/school links could take. We discussed what we believe are the significant criteria that shape any parent involvement. In doing this we recognised that all forms of parent involvement have a place. However, we would be less than honest if we did not make it clear that we believe that if we want parents to provide maximum support for their children, and if we want our schools to reflect the needs of the communities we work in, then we need to be working towards home/school initiatives which involve participation and partnership.

WHAT ARE THE BARRIERS TO PARTNERSHIP?

Before looking closely at practical ways in which we can involve parents as full participants in their children's education it is useful to consider some of the barriers to this participation.

PARENTS' NEGATIVE HISTORIES OF SCHOOLING

One common observation during our implementation of the TTALL program was that for many parents school does not hold good memories. While they may look back with fondness at the friends they made, their memories of teachers are mixed. Most parents can remember teachers they liked, but most can also remember those they did not like. The parents whom we see typically at P & C meetings and school functions are often those with more positive memories of teachers and schooling. As we introduced TTALL we found that the parents who had experienced problems with teachers were less trusting of schools, and reticent about becoming involved.

Rather than being threatened by this fact, teachers must take it into account when setting up parent initiatives. Parents will need to be convinced that the involvement will be an enjoyable experience, not a threatening and patronising one.

SOME PARENTS HAVE BEEN FAILURES WITHIN THE SCHOOL SYSTEM

While we as teachers would like to say that 'no child is ever a failure', the reality is that for some parents, school is not associated with being successful. Some have been in the bottom graded class, some have failed external exams, some spent all the primary years in the 'Wombats' reading group. Whether we like it or not, this is a significant barrier for some parents. In fact, in some cases, it is sufficient to keep parents away from school altogether. The following comments from two different TTALL parents show just how negative parent experiences can be:

> I can understand about self esteem. You know I spent most of my time writing out lines. One teacher would give me lines and then in the next class I'd get more. It was nothing for me to go home with 100–120 lines. How could I do my homework? I really hated school. I wasn't any good and Mum and Dad couldn't read so they couldn't help me.
>
> Shelley

> I hated school. They said I couldn't do the subject I wanted to 'cause I wasn't bright enough. I wasn't bad or anything but I just sat there.
> I couldn't wait to leave, so as soon as I did Year 4 (10) I left. I really wanted to do nursing or something but the school told me I wasn't clever enough.
>
> Lola

TEACHERS OFTEN SEE PARENTS AS A THREAT

It is fair to say that many teachers feel threatened by parents. This is hardly surprising. Some parents never come near a school until they perceive a problem in the practices of the teacher. As a result, when a parent requests a meeting with a teacher, most teachers start to worry. The problem is that this phenomenon needs to be considered in light of the above barriers. Furthermore, every teacher needs to ask him or herself: 'When was the last time I visited my child's school to say something positive?' Parents, like teachers, are busy people. Hence our contacts with schools tend to be for crisis management rather than genuine two-way communication.

The following comment made by a teacher in one of our TTALL schools shows just how threatened teachers can be:

That mother is there every afternoon just waiting to talk to me — every afternoon. I just try to avoid her. I am not having her work in my room. She is a pain.

Kindergarten Teacher

CHILDREN SOMETIMES DISCOURAGE THEIR PARENTS FROM BECOMING INVOLVED IN SCHOOL

While younger children would normally love to have their parents visit their school, some children as they grow older tend to discourage this involvement. While children do at times have problems with teachers, most are reluctant to have parents take complaints to the school. This is not surprising; children know that after the parent leaves the school they need to get on with their teachers.

Each of these barriers must be considered by teachers when attempting to involve parents as partners in their children's education. There are several important consequences for schools because of these barriers.

- If parents are to become more active participants in their children's education then teachers must take the initiative in the first instance. If schools do not attempt to do anything then clearly the barriers will remain.
- When gauging the response of parents to any school initiatives, teachers must do so in the light of the above barriers. That is, if few parents turn up for the first participatory workshop, don't be despondent; for some parents there is a history of negative feelings towards schools that needs to be broken down.
- When planning any initiative consider basic cultural factors. For example, for many parents formal meetings are not part of their culture. We should never be surprised when the majority of parents who attend a P & C meeting are the better educated parents, professional people, or those involved in other community groups. These are the people who understand what formal committee meetings are about. Some of them might even like them.
- In the light of the above, don't expect parent involvement to take off overnight. Sustained effort is required.

IMPLEMENTING A VARIETY OF PARTICIPATION INITIATIVES

In the rest of this chapter we want to explore the Participation Program options outlined as part of our description of Home/School Initiatives in Chapter 2 (pp. 20–2). It is by implementing some of these options that we begin to break down the barriers that create an artificial and damaging division between home and school. What we want to examine is how we can involve parents as partners in each of the following areas:
- school policies and procedures;
- curriculum information;
- classroom information;
- student feedback;
- parental support of their children.

SCHOOL POLICIES AND PROCEDURES

One of the frequent problems schools face is that they are often promoting educational ideas that are not part of the wider community's experience. As a result, most schools (in fact virtually all teachers) at some time are confronted by parents who question the literacy practices that are being implemented.

While schools can simply plough on with their practices and ignore parents, this is hardly productive. A much better approach is to involve parents in the development of literacy policies and procedures within the school. The following are just some of the ways to involve parents.
- When setting up school committees to develop new curriculum initiatives, include parent representation.
- Provide access to current educational debate in summary form for all parents. Schools might initiate a series of one-page 'Discussion Starters' on topics of interest, e.g. 'What is whole language?' 'What's a genre — do you eat it or spray it?' 'What's all the fuss about grammar?' 'Was there really a "Golden Age" when literacy standards were higher?'
- Involve parents in committees set up to purchase new books.

The above ideas are hardly new. Some readers will say, 'Yeah, I've tried all that and no-one is interested.' Our normal reply to this claim is to point out that while some parents do not show an active interest in broader educational issues, all will show interest if they can see how it has an impact upon their own children. Furthermore, there is no point providing some of the above opportunities if it is simply tokenistic involvement. Such strategies must be used within the context of a total commitment to parent participation. Parents will not participate if they perceive that their involvement is not genuinely wanted. One of the parents in the TTALL program described her early experiences as a school parent in this way:

> *Because my eldest is nearly 25, there was none of this sort of thing (TTALL) when he went to school. The schools weren't open to parents except on Education Day, and maybe Sports Day. You weren't encouraged to interfere. You couldn't go up and ask the teacher what was wrong, or how could you help or something. You were virtually told — you know — more or less, that we're the teacher, you're only the mother.*
>
> Lynne

CURRICULUM INFORMATION

While there is a place for information sheets, parent handbooks etc., most have little widespread effectiveness. The reality of our age is that most people lead busy lives. As a result most parents are very selective about the things they read. If leaflets and information booklets ever escape the fungus layer at the bottom of children's bags, they typically end up in the bin after a few neglected days on the kitchen table. Another reason for this fate is that information leaflets suffer from a number of key problems. Often they contain too much information. The language used frequently contains a great deal of jargon, and the tone is regularly patronising, e.g. 'Let us help you to be a better parent.' The design and layout is often of poor quality and the distribution method is usually poor. Would the average teacher like to see something important being delivered by a seven-year-old child?

If schools are serious about communicating curriculum information to parents, then other procedures are necessary. Once again, the school's desire to share curriculum information should be used as a valuable opportunity to involve parents and to find out about their needs. (See example overleaf.)

The development of community resource people is an effective way to achieve widespread awareness of curriculum initiatives. These people can be involved initially in the following ways:

- as participants in in-service activities planned for staff;
- as part of a literacy curriculum sub-committee set up within the school;
- as part of specific activities that relate to curriculum initiatives — for example, organising a school publishing company, purchasing early reading material, planning the M S Readathon, co-ordinating entries into writing competitions, compiling school writing anthologies, planning literacy enrichment activities for talented children.

VARDY'S ROAD PUBLIC SCHOOL

Vardy's Road, Seven Hills, NSW 2147
Telephones: (Primary) 624 3051, (Infants) 624 3278
PRINCIPAL: Mr. G. J. DOHERTY, B.Ec. Grad.Dip.Ed.St.
DEPUTY PRINCIPAL: Mrs. R. McKERIHAN, B.Ed.

27th April, 1989.

Dear Pam,

SCHOOL FORUM

Thank you for indicating your willingness to become involved in our School Forum. Our first meeting was to have been next Tuesday, but as I am required to attend a special Principals' Conference on that day, we will meet in the Staffroom from 3.00 to 4.00 p.m. on

THURSDAY, 4TH MAY

Parent Reps: Keith Whittington, Brian Staniland, Chris Collins,
                Janelle Willett, Marie Mathews, Narelle Rogerson,
                Renate Duncan

Teacher Reps: John Matis, Pam Lees, Pam Jennings, Pam Richardson,
                Helen Brangwin, Sue Franklin, Robyn McKerihan

At our first meeting we can discuss the details of how the Forum might function. Essentially, my idea is that this group of parents and teachers (and perhaps representatives from a Student Council?) will meet once a month to discuss school policy in the broadest sense.

It is not proposed that the Forum be a decision-making body, but it will necessarily influence decisions about Policy from a school management point of view and from a broad curriculum-development point of view.

It is hoped that the Forum will provide a semi-formal means of:

-   facilitating parent/teacher/executive interaction and
    co-operation;

-   increasing Community Involvement;

-   encouraging a wider input and diversity of ideas into
    the operation of the school.

Contd....

2.

Some of the issues that might be discussed could include:

- Fair Discipline Code (school uniforms and corporal punishment).

- Use of school facilities.

- Equipment, property and maintenance needs of the school.

- Open Days, displays, etc.

- Teaching and Testing the basic skills.

- Reporting to parents.

- Clarificiation of School Aims and Objectives.

- The learning environment.

- Government Initiatives, e.g. Multicultural Education, Bike Education, Non-Sexist Policy, Library Policy, Committees of Inquiry, etc.

- Technology in teaching and administration.

- Efficient Management and Accountability.

- Issues raised by parents, pupils and teachers.

- Annual Reports to the Education Department.

- Program Evaluations.

  Etc., Etc.

General Proposals:

- Forum chaired by persons other than Principal (Perhaps on a rotating basis).

- Minutes kept and available.

- Representatives report to Staff Meetings/P. & C. Meetings

- Advance Agenda open to everyone.

- Present teacher participation in decision-making to remain unaltered.

I'm looking forward to our first meeting. Hope you can attend.

All the best,

Greg

Greg Doherty

While only small numbers of parents can be involved in this way, ideally they can then be used as resource people in other contexts. For example, parents can report to P&C meetings, parent–teacher nights etc.

CLASSROOM INFORMATION

While it is possible to provide written details on classroom literacy programs and practices, one of the most effective ways to do this for parents who do not work during the day is to invite parents to visit classrooms to observe curriculum initiatives in action. The following are just some of the ideas that you might use.

- Ask parents to visit the classroom in Kindergarten to observe a shared reading session involving prediction. Provide them with a handout prior to the session with a list of key points to note as they observe. For example:
    - Notice how the children are encouraged to think about the meaning of the story (title, illustrations etc.) prior to the reading.
    - Take note of the way the children are encouraged to read the predictable parts of the text.
    - Observe the way the teacher points to the print to reinforce that words convey meaning.
    - Notice how important the illustrations are to help children understand the text.
    - Notice the questions the teacher asks about the book during and after the reading.

    Following such a session provide parents with a brief explanation of all that you were attempting to do. Stress the importance of such a strategy for reinforcing that reading is all about making meaning. Perhaps also provide some advice concerning suitable books for reading at home.
- Ask parents to visit your classroom to observe a writing session. Prior to the session provide a single page handout that explains what the children will be doing during the session. As well, provide them with a list of several things to observe (see example opposite).

    While parents who are not free during school hours are more difficult to involve it is still possible to provide similar activities to these at other hours. Small groups of children can by arrangement attend school at other times (e.g. 5.30–6.30 pm) to allow the same observational strategies to be used.

    Alternatively, video material can be used to allow specific literacy practices to be observed. Given the widespread use of video cameras in schools

OBSERVING A WRITING LESSON

My aim as a teacher is to help your child develop as a writer. I want him/her to be able to use writing for a variety of purposes. This means that they need to learn how to:

- organise their ideas;

- choose the right form to write it in;

- collect ideas and information if needed;

- revise their work;

- present it in an appropriate form for their readers.

In the lesson you will observe children involved in one of the following stages of the writing process:

- Organising their ideas for draft writing.

- Writing draft material.

- Working out the form their writing will take.

- Revising their work.

- Talking to other people about their writing prior to revision.

- Editing their work by checking spelling, punctuation and grammar.

- Preparing the final product.

Please try to find time to observe:

- What activity your child is involved in.

- How I as the teacher support the writers in the room.

In particular, take note of the questions I ask and the information I give them.

it may even be possible to videotape one of your own lessons. The advantage of this is that parents have the opportunity to observe their own children, something that all parents find interesting.

STUDENT FEEDBACK

All parents want feedback concerning their children's progress. Sadly, little specific feedback is given. In some schools the half-yearly and yearly reports are almost all that is offered. One of the problems with such feedback is that it is so infrequent and it provides little information. Once again, we favour forms of feedback which provide opportunities for parent involvement and genuine two-way communication. Below are some of the alternatives that we believe are useful.

Classroom participation

Strategies like those just described in Classroom Information are also useful because they provide parents with valuable opportunities to see their children participating in learning with other children. At times this can lead to the negative consequences of insensitive parental comparisons but, if handled sensitively, these opportunities are a powerful way to allow parents to learn how their children are coping with the demands of schooling.

Portfolios

Another important form of feedback is the use of Portfolios. While at times simply sending home students' school books is useful, a more systematic approach to the sharing of student work is preferable. One procedure for using Portfolios is as follows:

Step 1: Prepare a list of literacy work to be taken home. This might include:
- several examples of narrative writing (including drafts as well as the final product);
- samples of writing from other subjects, e.g. a report from science, notes made on a video, an excursion assignment;
- a list of frequently misspelt words;
- a text that the child has chosen to read to his/her parents;
- a list of books read up to now (such a list might include the title, author and date completed);
- a self-evaluation prepared by the child.

Step 2: Involve each child in preparing the Portfolios. Explain the purpose of the work samples to the students.

PORTFOLIO 1

Dear Parent,

Attached is a sample of your child's literacy work in the past 4 weeks. The sample includes:

- Two stories (draft and published work).

- Three pieces of writing from other subjects.

- A list of words that your child needs help with.

- A book which they will read to you.

- A list of books read in the last four weeks.

The purpose of the work sample is to keep you informed about the work your child is completing and to help you to gauge progress.

Please use the sample as an opportunity to praise your child's efforts. You might also use it to offer help where problems are evident.

If you have any questions about the work sample or your child's progress please let me know.

Sincerely,

Ms Grace

Step 3: Send the Portfolio home. Make sure its purpose is outlined, and that you include procedures for parents to follow up any of the material contained in it.

Step 4: Provide time for parents to visit the school to discuss the Portfolio.

PARENTAL SUPPORT OF THEIR CHILDREN

This final category is the focus for the rest of this book. Ultimately, the most vital form of parent involvement is in the specific literacy activities of children.

As we pointed out in Chapter 1, parents have a critical role to play as supporters of their children's learning. While we will describe a number of major parent participation programs in the next chapter and will follow that with a description of the TTALL program, there are many other starting points for parent involvement.

In a sense it does not matter how you involve parents as long as the following points are observed.

1 Parents must not be involved simply to fulfil the school's purposes.
2 The starting point for parent programs must be a sense of partnership, of accepting that each has much to learn from the other.
3 The overriding purpose must be to bring about positive literacy benefits for children.
4 All strategies must consider the needs of parents.
5 All initiatives should lead parents to assume greater involvement in their children's learning.
6 Wherever possible, parent expertise and knowledge should be used.

Given these basic principles, there are many starting points for parent involvement in the support of their children. Each of these initiatives represents one way to take a first step towards significant partnership programs. It is our belief that from these simple beginnings can emerge genuine partnership which ultimately will lead to the initiation of contacts by parents, not just the school. The following are just some of the starting points that we have found successful.

Paired Reading

Paired Reading is a useful way to start because it immediately offers a strategy for parents to read with their children. This simple technique was first designed by Morgan (1976) and was later refined by Tizard, Schofield and Hewison (1982), Topping and McKnight (1984), and Topping and Wolfendale (1985). It involves two phases. The first is a simultaneous phase where a tutor and child sit next to each other, reading out loud together. The tutor adjusts the reading speed to that of the child. Miscues are picked up as the reading proceeds; the child is asked to repeat the correct word before proceeding.

The second independent reading phase involves a similar pattern of synchronised reading, except the reader attempts independent reading when confident. This is achieved by encouraging the child to gently tap the tutor when he/she feels that it is possible to read independently. The tutor praises the child and he/she proceeds until an error is made. This is then corrected by the tutor reading the original version. The reading then proceeds in a synchronised way until the child again signals to the tutor for independent reading to begin.

The studies that have employed this strategy have been highly successful. Positive results have been found with diverse school communities covering all socioeconomic backgrounds (Topping, in Topping & Wolfendale, 1985; Turner, 1987).

A good way to introduce this strategy is to invite parents to your classroom to take part in a Paired Reading session. Before the session provide a description of the Paired Reading technique. When the parents visit your classroom allow them first to observe you using the technique with a child. At the end of this demonstration allow time for parents to ask questions about the technique and its benefits. Following this discussion have all parents try the technique with their children. While they use Paired Reading, wander around observing them and answering their questions.

Using editing checklists

Using editing checklists (see example overleaf) is one practical way to introduce parents to forms of writing support beyond correction. The editing checklist should be designed to meet the specific needs of each child.

Before asking parents to help their children to use an editing checklist invite them to either an in-school writing lesson, or an after-school parent session focusing on writing.

If the in-school option is used, demonstrate the use of editing checklists for the children and their parents. The best way to conduct such a demonstration is to use a piece of your own writing on an overhead projector and an editing checklist that you have designed for the purposes of the demonstration.

Following this demonstration, all children should work through their own piece of writing using an editing checklist that you have provided. Parents should be encouraged to help their children as they engage in this task. After this session parents can be encouraged to help their children to use similar procedures at home. This should be followed up 3–4 weeks later with an after-school session at which parents can ask about the process that has been used.

If the after-school session is used to introduce this strategy, then a similar demonstration of the use of editing checklists should be conducted with the parents. While this is a little more threatening for parents (especially for those who are not strong in literacy) it can still be useful if done sensitively. The

---

EDITING CHECKLIST

When revising your work look for the following things:

* Have I used a logical sequence of ideas or facts?

* Does the piece start in such a way that the reader will want to read on?

* Check sentence beginnings. Have I varied them?

* Have I used commas in the right places?

* Has paragraphing been used?

* Use your list of common spelling errors to check your work?

* Read it out loud to someone else.

---

procedure is very similar to the in-school procedure, in that the teacher demonstrates using a piece of his/her writing and an editing checklist. However, instead of involving children in the process parents are invited to comment on the piece as the checklist is used.

As with Paired Reading the use of editing checklists as a starting point for parent involvement has three main advantages. First, it has the immediate benefit that it involves parents in the literacy activities of their children. Second, it provides parents with an insight into the teacher's literacy practices. Third, it provides parents with an opportunity to respond to classroom practices and indicate some of the priorities they see as important in literacy.

PAIRED READING

This is a simple method for reading with your child. It has been shown to be an effective way to help children develop as readers. When using it follow the following steps:

Step 1   Ask your child to choose a book that they would like to read.

Step 2   Explain that you're going to do some Paired Reading.

Step 3   Sit alongside your child with them holding the book. Point out to your child that you are going to read the book out loud with them following.

Step 4   Begin reading adjusting your pace to suit your child. Words that are missed by the child are repeated by them in correct form, then they read on.

                Read for 5-10 minutes per day.

Step 5   After confidence has been achieved with the above (1 to 3 weeks) introduce the second stage of Paired Reading.

                This is similar to the first stage except the reader attempts to read alone when confident. Begin reading together but encourage your child to tap you when they wish to read alone. You praise the child then he/she reads till a miscue is made. This is corrected and both read on till the child again feels confident to read alone.

Step 6   Increase periods of reading up to 15 minutes.

Step 7   Stop using this technique when the child becomes bored with it or when progress is so great that it is no longer needed.

Home reading programs

Home reading programs are conducted by many schools. However, frequently they fail to go far enough. In many instances such programs are little more that a sheet for parents to sign to say they have heard their child read a basal reader. We believe that home reading programs should involve much more. The following represent what we see as the steps to a successful home reading program; see facing page for examples of grids for parents.

Step 1: Explain to parents the purposes of a home reading program. This may be done by asking parents to visit the school to take part in an introductory workshop, or could be done through a leaflet. The latter is the least successful. If it must be used we suggest that it be mailed to all parents to create greater impact and to ensure that all parents receive it at the same time. When outlining the purpose the teacher should explain why it is worthwhile, what their role is as parents, and what is expected of the child. The sample below shows how these issues were outlined for parents as part of the TTALL Community Tutor Program.

Step 2: Demonstrate how parents should listen to and read with their children. This should cover how parents listen, ask questions, prompt, follow up errors etc. Ideally this should be done as part of the introductory workshop. If this occurs, a demonstration should be given involving a child from the class. As well as this, parents should be provided with concise hints on how to read with their children. As part of the TTALL Community Tutor Program all parents received basic hints on listening to their children reading.

Step 3: Parents should be provided with assistance concerning the choice of reading material. While the home reading program may involve the supply of the books from school, ideally our aim should be to help parents and children make appropriate choices themselves. Options for achieving this are providing a list of book titles suitable for specific ages, and mounting book displays as part of parent-teacher functions.

Step 4: Parents should be provided with a simple record keeping system for home reading.

Step 5: Plan special book celebrations. These events are opportunities for parents and children to come together to share some of their home reading experiences. Ideas for such an event include:

• Reader's theatre which involves a group of children reading dramatically a play or dialogue (in script form);

SHARING TIME

By reading, talking and listening to your children, and by sharing books, you are actively helping your child to learn to read.

📖 Reading aloud ....

Children love to hear a story read with

☆   emotion
☆   invented sound effects
☆   different voices
☆   funny faces
☆   changes in the volume of your voice - loud, soft and in between

It's a good idea to practise reading the story before you perform.

Talk about the story or illustrations but don't spoil the book.

Sometimes talk about:

☆   The part of the story you both enjoyed
☆   The feelings you both had after reading the book. Sometimes it's funny, boring, sad, scary ....
☆   What you both thought about the story or the main character

SOMETIMES, NOTHING NEEDS TO BE SAID

WHERE DO WE START?

Relax .....   With young children, take the opportunity to give them a cuddle, or sit them on your knee while you read to them.

Time .....   Find a time which is suitable to both you and your children. Reading time should be an enjoyable experience not a duty.

Selection ....   Give your child a chance to choose a book to read. Children need to have some control over what they want to read. However, don't be afraid to help them out now and again.

Encourage ..   Let your child be in control of the book. Make sure they can SEE the pictures and the words. Allow them to turn the pages, if they want.

Sometimes children like to join in reading the story.

- Book sharing groups which are organised in age groups, author groups, specific book groups, or genre groups (adventure stories, science fiction, non-fiction, fantasy, legends);
- Book parades (for younger children) in which children dress as special characters;
- Visiting authors and illustrators who are often willing to run workshops in schools and can provide a valuable focus for parent participation.

Step 6: Once the program is running you should provide a follow-up meeting, or a follow-up letter, to find out how the program is working. If this is a planned meeting at school you might go over the details of the program, demonstrate reading with a child, or provide a time for questions and answers.

If approached in this way we believe that home reading programs have the potential to create positive links between the school and home.

Listening to My Child Read ...

Golden Rules:

☆ **Always be positive.**
☆ **Be patient.**
☆ **Praise their efforts.**
☆ **Make it a pleasurable time.**

Let's begin ...

☆ Listening to your child should be an enjoyable, shared experienced
☆ Find a time when you and your child are relaxed - make it a special time.
☆ Sit beside your child, either at a table or on the couch. Allow your child to hold the book.
☆ Don't argue with or force your child to read, if they are tired or disinterested; there is no pleasure for either person.
☆ Patience is extremely important as reading aloud can be difficult, especially if the child is frightened about making mistakes.
☆ Keep your sessions brief, about 10 minutes, no more than 15 minutes.

Let's read ...

Talk to your child/ren about the book before they start

☆ Look at front and back cover, the illustrations, the author.
☆ Sometimes ask what they think the story will be about. Talking about the book helps to create an interest in the story.

Let's listen ....

Remember .... PATIENCE ......

What to do when children read.

☆ Everyone makes mistakes when they read and its more obvious when we are nervous.

So what about 'mistakes'?

☆ It's best if you correct as few mistakes as possible while your child is reading.

The only mistakes corrected are those which stop the child from understanding the meaning of the story or sentence.

 PAUSE: After your child makes a mistake PAUSE, there is a chance your child will correct it.

 PROMPT: If your child doesn't self-correct, then tell him/her the word.
(See diagram for other ways of helping your child)

 PRAISE: The most important thing is to keep encouraging your child to try for themselves and to praise them when they succeed.

RESEARCH WRITING

The final example is one that has proven very popular with parents. As any parent will testify, when the request for the first project of the year arrives at home, most adult hearts sink because they know that a series of painful sessions are about to commence with their child. When trips to the library are added, one can easily understand why most parents hate projects.

For this reason, most parents respond positively to any suggestion that aims to equip their children for the demanding task of research. This is a parent involvement initiative which will require several workshops either during school time or after school with the children in attendance (see Cairney & Munsie, 1992c for more details). It involves a number of structured steps designed to enable parents to provide their children with support.

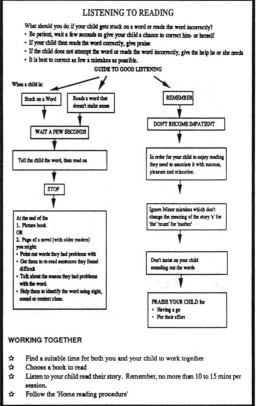

READING AT HOME

No. 3

Learning to read is one of the most important achievements of your child's schooling.

It is important for you to encourage, support and show an interest in your child/ren's reading, throughout their school years.

What Can Parents Do?

The home is just as important as school in developing a love, interest and understanding of reading.

☆ Reading with your children helps them understand that print on the page has a message, adds to their vocabulary and gives them an enjoyment of stories.

☆ As children learn to read by themselves, they need time for quiet sustained silent reading. The amount of time should be for as long as the child is able to maintain interest in the story. *Ten minutes each day* is better than 30 minutes per week,

Some simple steps to follow:

• Let your child/ren choose the book they want to read but make sure it is within their reading ability.
• Encourage reluctant readers to finish the books they start
• Talk to them about the story, even while you work in the kitchen. You could suggest:
  - What was the story about?
  - Tell me the part you enjoyed the most.

LISTENING TO READING

What should you do if your child gets stuck on a word or reads the word incorrectly?
• Be patient, wait a few seconds to give your child a chance to correct him- or herself
• If your child then reads the word correctly, give praise
• If the child does not attempt the word or reads the word incorrectly, give the help he or she needs
• It is best to correct as few mistakes as possible.

GUIDE TO GOOD LISTENING

When a child is:

| Stuck on a Word | Reads a word that doesn't make sense |

REMEMBER

WAIT A FEW SECONDS

DON'T BECOME IMPATIENT

Tell the child the word, then read on

In order for your child to enjoy reading they need to associate it with success, pleasure and relaxation.

STOP

Ignore Minor mistakes which don't change the meaning of the story 'a' for 'the' 'mum' for 'mother'

At the end of the
1. Picture book
OR
2. Page of a novel (with older readers) you might:
• Point out words they had problems with
• Get them to re-read sentences they found difficult
• Talk about the reason they had problems with the word.
• Help them to identify the word using sight, sound or context clues.

Don't insist on your child sounding out the words

PRAISE YOUR CHILD for
• Having a go
• For their effort

WORKING TOGETHER

☆ Find a suitable time for both you and your child to work together
☆ Choose a book to read
☆ Listen to your child read their story. Remember, no more than 10 to 15 mins per session.
☆ Follow the 'Home reading procedure'

CTP Programme: UWS , Nepean, Copyright Cairney & Munsie

Step 1: Arrange a first meeting in which the following activities take place.
• Discuss the reason for project work (i.e. development of research skills, reading and writing skills, development of specific knowledge).
• Discuss problems associated with project work, e.g. lack of resources, children copying material from books.
• Introduce a simple research cycle like the one shown below.
• Explain the elements of the cycle and show some finished research work.
• Demonstrate topic selection and ask parents and their children to choose their own from within a limited topic area, e.g. a country of the world, a sport, a famous person, an animal.
• Demonstrate free writing for the groups then encourage them to try it.

HOME READING DIARY

NAME: _____

Reading at home

Some hints ....

- Read for 5 to 15 minutes each day

- Arrange a regular time which suits you and your child and keep to it

- Choose a special place with no interruptions eg. TV, other family members

- Make it an enjoyable time for both the child and yourself

- There are a number of ways to encourage reading at home. You may like to vary your reading methods, according to the needs of your child.

    a) Paired Reading : Read out loud together (See Reading Handbook)

    b) The child reads to you. Give praise and encouragement. Prompt when the child needs assistance. (See Parent Handbook, *Pause, Prompt, Praise*)

    c) Read to your child

Ideally, both parents and children should try this. Some sensitivity may be needed in the cases of parents who have limited literacy skills.

- Help participants to formulate a series of questions to guide the rest of their research work. If a simpler procedure is required, restrict participants to a single broad topic area (e.g. famous people). This makes it easier to devise a common set of questions. Ask the participants to come back to the next session with three pieces of reference material (if possible) for their topic.

- Finish this session by explaining that next time they will begin work on a report. Show them a report and explain some of its characteristics.

    NOTE: This session will require about 90 minutes.

Step 2: About one week later, hold a second workshop. This workshop covers the following.

- Ask participants to share with others their success, or lack of it, in obtaining reference material.

- Suggest strategies for overcoming any problems identified.

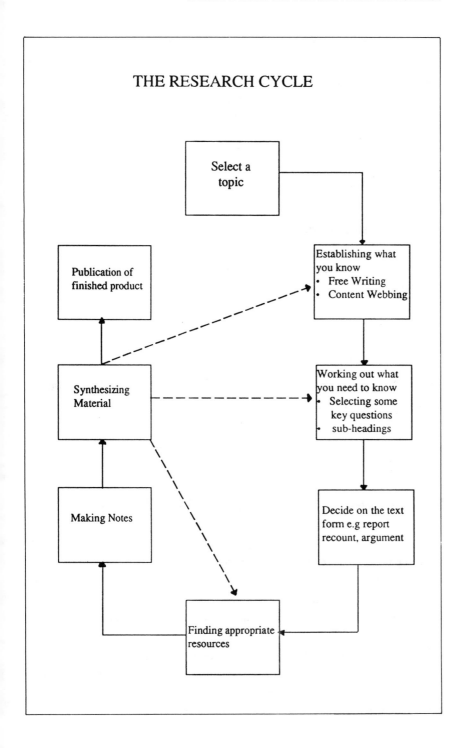

THE RESEARCH CYCLE

Select a topic

Establishing what you know
- Free Writing
- Content Webbing

Publication of finished product

Synthesizing Material

Working out what you need to know
- Selecting some key questions
- sub-headings

Making Notes

Decide on the text form e.g report recount, argument

Finding appropriate resources

- Explain that you wish to proceed with the research process. Show the group the research cycle once again and revise the various steps. Show them where they are up to.
- Using your own topic as a starting point, and references collected in advance, demonstrate basic note making.

Note Making Hints

- Avoid copying out 'slabs' of material from reference books.

- Write ideas as clearly and concisely as you can in your own words. Whole sentences are not necessary.

- Separate each point to make it easier to cut and paste and connect ideas later.

- Keep a record of all references you use including title, author, publisher, place of publication and year published.

- Perfect spelling is not necessary for note making but copy special words and names carefully.

- Make a note of the location of useful diagrams, maps, illustrations etc.

- Have participants attempt to make notes.
- Demonstrate how you turn notes into connected writing. You might show them how to use colour coding, cut and paste or other systems.
- Talk about the need to find extra material if you find gaps once you combine notes.
- Finish the session by talking about the last few steps in the research cycle and suggesting that all return to the next session with their notes turned into a draft of their research.

  NOTE: This session requires about 90 minutes.

Step 3: The purpose of this session is to examine the final steps in the research writing process. This will include the following.

- Talk about problems experienced in turning notes into connected text. Attempt to address the various problems raised.
- Review the research cycle and discuss the steps that still need to be completed.
- Demonstrate the use of illustrations and diagrammatic material using your own example.
- Provide an opportunity for questions and answers.
- Outline the steps still to be completed in the research process.

  NOTE: This session requires about 30–60 minutes.

Step 4: The final step in this process can be achieved in one of two ways. Ideally there should be an opportunity for children and parents to bring the completed work to school to share. This session is basically a celebration of authorship and a chance to review the whole process.

If parents cannot attend, the session could take place with the children only, during normal lesson time. Parents would then be sent a final letter thanking them for being involved in the process and inviting them to contact you if they require any extra help.

MOVING BEYOND FIRST STEPS

All the ideas given in this chapter are seen as just some of the ways of initiating parent partnership. These initial activities are meant to be the starting point of significant parent/school partnerships, rather than ends in themselves. In the next chapter we examine how other people throughout Australia have initiated such programs.

4

Parent initiatives from around the world

As we have already stressed in Chapters 2 and 3, parent involvement in children's education is obviously an important element in effective schooling (Epstein, 1983; Delgado-Gaitan, 1991). There appears to be a high positive correlation between parent knowledge, beliefs, and interactive styles, with children's school achievement. Attempts to address this important relationship have varied. However, a number have reflected deficit models, and have been based on the assumption that some children receive 'good' or 'appropriate' preparation for schooling, while others receive 'poor' or 'inappropriate' preparation. This view has been criticised because of its failure to recognise that schooling is a cultural practice (Auerbach, 1989). What it ignores, is the fact that much of the variability of student achievement in school reflects discrepancies that exist between school resources and instructional methods, and the cultural practices of the home (Au & Kawakami, 1984; Cazden, 1988; Heath, 1983; Moll, 1988).

Schools engage in specific discourses and hence inconsistently tap the social and cultural resources of society, privileging specific groups by emphasising particular linguistic styles, curricula, and authority patterns (Bourdieu, 1977). To be a teacher in any school demands specific ways of using language, behaving, interacting, and adherence to sets of values and attitudes (Gee, 1990). There is obvious potential for mismatches between these discourses and those which have been characteristic of some children's homes and communities. It would seem that those children who enter school, already having been partially apprenticed into the social practices of schooling (of which literacy is a part), invariably perform better at the practices of schooling right from the start. Our literacy definitions are inevitably reflective of a specific ideology, and as a consequence, arbitrarily advantage some while disadvantaging others (Freire & Macedo, 1987; Lankshear & Lawler, 1987; Street, 1984).

But how does one respond to the cultural mismatches of home and school? Should one focus on developing initiatives that provide parents with the cultural practices that enable them to cope with the limited practices of the school (Lareau, 1991), or find ways to help schools recognise the cultural practices of the home and community and build effective communication between these parties (Delgado-Gaitan, 1992)? Obviously the answer is "yes" to both of these possibilities.

Involving parents more closely in school or preschool education has the potential to develop new understanding by each party of the other's specific cultural practices. This may well enable both teachers and parents to understand the way each defines, values and uses literacy. In this way schooling can be adjusted to meet the needs of families, and parents in turn can also be given the opportunity to observe and understand the definitions of literacy that schools support, and which ultimately empower individuals to take their place in society.

A recurring theme in the recent literature is that parents must be viewed as equal partners, and that there must be a reciprocal relationship. As Kruger & Mahon (1990, p. 4) point out, "parental involvement in literacy learning has much greater value than as an add-on to what teachers do". Harry (1992) argues that such parent initiatives must forge collaborative relationships that create mutual understanding between parents and teachers—a "posture of reciprocity"—and which are associated with a shift from the school to parents and the community.

In essence, what some of these educators are arguing for is not the transmission of knowledge from schools to parents and their children, but rather a process of reaching mutual consensus between the partners. This process of reaching shared understanding is what Vygotsky called "intersubjectivity" (1978). It involves a shared focus of attention and mutual understanding of any joint activity. Fitzgerald and Goncu (In press) suggest that this requires reaching agreement on the selection of activities, their goals, and plans for reaching the goals. At this stage in the development of parent initiatives there are few programs operating which could claim to have achieved the type of shared understanding and purpose that is being advocated. In spite of this many have developed innovative programs that go some way towards developing genuine partnership.

WHAT FORM HAVE FAMILY LITERACY INITIATIVES TAKEN?

Attempts to involve families more fully in their children's literacy learning have taken many forms. Even the labelling of these programs has been diverse. Throughout this book we have talked of "parent initiatives" in a fairly generic sense to cover work that could also have been termed family, community or intergenerational literacy. This use of overlapping terms has created some degree of confusion. As Nickse (p. 35, 1993) points out, there has been a "... strange mix of titles and names. ..." A second order confusion has been the addition of the words "involvement", "participation" and "partnership" to the major term. We need to consider more fully what we mean by 'being involved', 'participant', 'family', 'parent', 'partnership' and even 'community'? Does participation lead to partnership? Not necessarily. These are just some of the questions concealed by the use of these terms (see Cairney, In press for a more detailed discussion).

There have been many attempts to design parent programs, most have been focussed on parents with preschool or primary aged children. Some of the most significant early initiatives in this area occurred in the United Kingdom. The Plowden report (Department of Education and Science, 1967) was one of a number of factors which probably influenced the significant number of initiatives. This report argued strongly for the concept of partnership between home and school. Many of the early programs focussed on the need to offer parents a limited range of reading strategies to use with their children. One of the most commonly used was the Paired Reading technique. This simple technique (discussed in Chapter 3) was first designed by Morgan (1976) and was later refined by Tizard, Schofield and Hewison (1982), Topping & McKnight (1984), and Topping & Wolfendale (1985). Some more recent programs in Australia have also utilised this strategy.

A number of the most successful British programs were designed for parents whose children have reading problems. While some of the programs showed encouraging outcomes, there was a degree of inconsistency. For example, the Haringey Reading Project found that some of the children whose parents were involved in their program made significant gains in reading achievement (irrespective of reading ability), while others made little (Tizard, Schofield, & Hewison; 1982).

In the United States there have been numerous attempts to design programs that aim to involve parents more fully in their children's literacy learning. Nickse (1993) has estimated that there are more than 500 programs in existence in the USA. However, she points out that evidence concerning their effectiveness is modest. The major source of funding for these programs has been from a variety of State and Federal government programs including *Head Start*, *Even Start*, and the *Family School Partnership Program*.

While it is encouraging that there have been a number of significant parent initiatives in many different countries in the past decade, our goal must be to see parent involvement grow to the point where parents and teachers do share responsibility as equal partners.

There appear to be three major arguments concerning the need for parental involvement in children's schooling. The first is the overwhelming evidence of the powerful effects of parents as their children's first teacher. Research suggests that programs are more likely to be successful when they are designed with high expectations for parent involvement, and when they accommodate the needs and perceptions of the particular families involved (Eastman 1988). Parents should share responsibility because they and their children's teachers are mutually accountable (Wolfendale, 1985 in Topping and Wolfendale, 1985)

The second reason for parent involvement in their children's schooling is concerned with the parents' rights and wishes to be involved. Advocates of this position in recent years argue that it is the duty of the school to liaise with and inform the parents of their children's schooling (Pugh, in Topping and Wolfendale, 1985).

The third reason, which has been discussed above, is that it is only by bringing parents and schools 'closer together' that we can hope to see shared understanding and mutual responsiveness develop. If we involve teachers in the community, and the community (including parents) in the school or preschool, then we open up the potential for "intersubjectivity" to develop.

PROGRAMS THAT PROVIDE STRATEGY-BASED PROGRAMS FOR PARENTS

The following are a number of well known programs that have been developed in Australia, the United States and the United Kingdom which provide some sense of the diversity of initiatives being implemented around the world.

SCHOOLS REACHING OUT (SRO)   INSTITUTE FOR RESPONSIVE EDUCATION

While this program is not specifically focussed on literacy, its outcomes have direct relevance for the learning of literacy. SRO is essentially an attempt to help urban public schools change their relationships with low-income parents and their communities. In doing so, it is hoped that children will achieve enhanced success academically and socially.

The Program: This initiative has grown from two pilot schools to almost 100 schools which are referred to collectively as the national League of Schools Reaching Out. SRO is a framework for action rather than a set program. It starts with a commitment to develop partnership between a school and its community and follows a sequence of logical steps which include: setting a common goal; developing an agenda of tasks to achieve; recognising the contribution of each member of the partnership; developing a shared language and basis for partnership; seeking the assistance of an outside facilitator; setting in place a problem solving process; working out how to share resources; allowing participants to self select; working towards the development of multiple voices.

Focus of the Program: The focus of the project is very much on individual schools which develop an agenda for the development of partnerships with their communities.

Age group of children: Elementary school children

Parent Group: Urban low income families

Availability : Institute for Responsive Education, Boston

PARTNERS IN LITERACY   LYNDA PEARCE

This program is essentially an inservice programme for support teachers, teachers and educators interested in parental involvement in reading projects developed by Lynda Pearce in Cambridge elementary schools in England. It was developed in response to specific student literacy needs.

The Program: This program is designed for teachers, and consists of a series of inservice activities based around eight separate booklets for parents, and a variety of associated activities and resources. The program involves an initial period of 6 weeks, is individualised, and varies according to the child's needs. It begins with an initial meeting between the support teacher, class teacher, parents and the child. Tasks are then selected for the three participants under the guidance of the support teacher. The class teacher is responsible for the daily programme in school and for selecting the most appropriate words, books, spellings, written work.

Focus of the Program: The program has been designed to develop a coordinated strategy for children with literacy difficulties which involves the child, the parent and the teacher. Essentially, it show teachers how they can provide the parents of children who have literacy difficulties with a range of strategies to use with their children at home.

Age group of children: Children aged 5 to 12 years

Parent Group: Parents of children experiencing literacy difficulties

Availability : Learning Development Aids, England

READ WITH ME   SUSAN HILL, UNIVERSITY OF SOUTH AUSTRALIA

Read with Me was developed in a disadvantaged school with parents, over a two year period with International Literacy Year funding. It was influenced strongly by Susan Hill's stated belief that parents with long term unemployment and poverty do not respond to simplistic approaches to literacy learning.

The Program: Two workshops are built around a video and an attractively presented parent book. The focus of the program is to share ideas on the ways parents read with their children. The video and book demonstrate shared reading in a non threatening way.

Parents who are non readers are given strategies to join in with their children as they read. The video and parent book adopt a non transmission approach where the positive interactions occurring in the home are encouraged.

Focus of the Program: This program has been designed to increase parents' confidence as they read with their children. The program is held in the homes of participants. Parents talk about and demonstrate some of the strategies they could use with their children

   Age group of children: 4 to 8 years

   Parent Group: Parents with limited literacy skills.

   Availability : Susan Hill, University of South Australia

PROJECT FLAME   TIMOTHY SHANAHAN & FLORA V. RODRIGUEZ-BROWN

Project FLAME is designed to provide literacy training and support to Hispanic, limited English proficient (LEP) parents to improve their ability to assist their children's literacy and future academic achievement.

The Program: The program attempts to provide training and support to change attitudes and improve abilities of LEP parents to use literacy and language in order to influence their children's literacy. It attempts to teach parents to locate and select appropriate books, magazines and other literacy materials; increase the availability of literacy materials in the home; and increase the amount of library use by families. In effect it aims to increase parent literacy and encourage them to draw attention to their use of literacy to the attention of their children.

Focus of the Program: Parents attend twice weekly ESL classes. They also attend parents as teachers classes twice a month. They are also invited to become involved in less structured meetings. Some sessions require them to work with their children.

   Age group of children: Children are of variable age.

   Parent Group: Hispanic parents with limited English proficiency

   Availability: Additional information from Timothy Shanahan and Flora V. Rodriguez-Brown, University of Illinois at Chicago.

PARENTS AS TUTORS PROGRAM   INNER CITY SCHOOL SUPPORT CENTRE, MINISTRY OF EDUCATION AND TRAINING, VICTORIA, AUSTRALIA

The **Parents as Tutors** program is a joint initiative of the Inner City Support Centre, the Disadvantaged Schools Program and the Brash Foundation. It aims to assist parents support their children.

The Program: The six week program involves sessions that consider the parents' role in children's learning; preparation for reading; the reading and writing processes; communication with the school; review and discussion of PAT program; and exploring further opportunities support for parents.

Focus of the Program: The *PAT* Program aims to provide parents with practical strategies for working with children at home. It also provides opportunities for parents to share their ideas and experiences with other parents. The program gives 'hands on training' for parents and others in the student support network eg community workers and teachers in the area of literacy development. Parents have been involved as participants and have also had input into the developing education program.

Age Group of Children: Pre school to Year 12

Parent Group: Parents from preschool to early secondary. This also includes parents from other language groups.

Availability : Ministry of Education and Training, Victoria, Australia.

EFFECTIVE PARTNERS IN SECONDARY LITERACY LEARNING (EPISLL)   TREVOR CAIRNEY & LYNNE MUNSIE

The EPISLL program developed out of the TTALL program (see Chapter 5). It was initiated at the request of a group of parents who had taken part in the TTALL program when their children were in Elementary school and who now wanted support because their children had reached secondary school. It is essentially a parent support program that is run as a series of interactive workshops.

The Program: The program consists of 11 two hour interactive workshops which are run over a period of 6 weeks. Each session ends with a hometask which normally involves parents talking or working with one of their children, or engaging in specific literacy practices. The content of the program covers the importance of positive relationships, setting realistic personal goals, learning, the nature of the reading and writing processes, strategies for assisting with their work (eg, summarising, notetaking, understanding the text book), organising time for study and strategies for researching information, locating and using community resources and the use of computers for word processing.

Focus of the Program: The focus is on providing parents with access to literacy practices that are related closely to success in schooling, and helping them to assist their children to gain control over these same practices.

Age Group of Children: Aged 12 to 17 years.

Parent Group: Parents of children in the secondary school from low income communities.

Availability : Trevor Cairney, University of Western Sydney Nepean, Australia

PARENTS AS TEACHERS   MISSOURI DEPARTMENT OF ELEMENTARY AND SECONDARY EDUCATION

The Program: The *Parents as Teachers* program is a comprehensive parenting program first developed by the Missouri Department of Elementary and Secondary Education to "demonstrate the value of high-quality parent education and family support."

Focus of the Program: The program is designed to provide support to parents to help them enhance their children's development from birth to age three years. It involves the development of a long term relationship with parents who meet in groups to discuss their children's development and to receive information on children's language, as well as intellectual, social and motor development. Parents are offered monthly meetings, home visits and written material. They are also encouraged to attend Health Department centres for regular developmental and health advice and check ups for their children.

Age Group of Children: Birth to 3 years

Parent Group: Parents with children aged Birth to 3 years

Availability : Missouri Department of Elementary and Secondary education and other agencies that have adopted the program

One of the things that is exciting about the above programs is that each attempts to provide comprehensive support for parents and children. While it can be seen that the programs have different purposes and target groups, all attempt to involve parents as partners in their children's education. Some are school focussed, while others are community based. All however, have the potential to lead to the "posture of reciprocity" which Harry (1992) argues such parent initiatives must forge. Nevertheless, programs like the above are simply starting points for the development of partnerships which will lead to significant and lasting changes to the nature of the relationship between schools and parents.

In the chapter that follows we will provide even more detailed information on one such initiative to provide readers with further guidance when designing parent initiatives that lead to collaboration and partnership.

5

The 'Talk To A Literacy Learner' experience

In setting up the TTALL program we were aware of the need to help parents interact more effectively with their children. That is, we wanted parents to respond to their children's reading and writing in such a way that their chances of success at school were maximised. In taking this approach we were attempting to help parents recapture the spontaneity that they were able to show when interacting with their young children as they first learnt to speak. We had observed that when children reached school age and literacy became the focus, parents seemed to change the role they played.

Upon entry to school, many parents cease to provide a risk-free environment in which children are encouraged to explore and solve problems, try out new skills and experience new things. Instead, many children seem to experience an environment where literacy skills are practised out of context, without the focus on meaning and without risk-taking.

In designing this program, we wanted to accept parents as full participants in their children's learning. To do this we decided to focus on the adult rather than the child. It was our aim to treat the parents as learners and to support them as they worked with their children. If children are to be given the chance to succeed, then parents need to become life-long supporters of their learning.

Our aim was to design an educational program which was concerned with both reading and writing, and which sought to:
- raise parental participation in the literacy activities of their children;
- change the nature of interactions adults have with their children;
- train community resource people who could be deployed in a wide range of community literacy activities;
- raise community expectations about literacy;
- serve as a catalyst for a variety of community-based literacy initiatives.

STAGE 1 OF THE TTALL PROGRAM

The program was originally developed for use at Lethbridge Park Primary and Lethbridge Park Preschool. While the programs were developed by the authors, the submission for funding and the ongoing operation of the project was supported by a large team of parents, school executive and teachers from the primary and pre-schools. Funding for the project was provided by the NSW Ministry for Education and Youth Affairs as part of International Literacy Year. Trials of the program were also funded in the Newcastle area at Stockton Preschool and Primary Schools.

Lethbridge Park is situated in the sprawling western suburbs of Sydney. It is an area which faces many of the problems associated with high density urban living, including isolation, and high rates of unemployment, marriage break-down, and single-parent families. Low educational participation, drug problems and vandalism are also common.

However, the initial support for the program by the community was encouraging. The parents were invited to consider involvement in the program from a series of written notices sent to all parents from Lethbridge Park Primary and Preschool. This was accompanied by extensive media coverage from both the Sydney and local media. After several weeks of advertising a public meeting was organised to explain the program. A simple information sheet was distributed requesting an indication of interest.

Fifty people attended the first meeting. From this group, 25 accepted an invitation to be involved in the program for a total of 16 two-hour sessions conducted two days per week over 8 weeks. In Stockton where the program was replicated 70 parents joined the program.

Parents indicated a variety of reasons for participating. For example, Paige wrote:

I would like to be able to help my children as much as I can when they start school. I would like to know the right way to go about school work.

Irena commented:

I realise there are new methods being used since I was taught and I wanted to know how to help my children more as I see them struggling in literacy.

Parents involved in our programs nominated a variety of times. For example, our first group nominated to attend the program 9–11 am each Monday and Wednesday. Parents who attended subsequent courses run at Lethbridge Park also elected to attend morning sessions. At Stockton Preschool and Primary School a day and evening program was used.

OVERVIEW OF THE PROGRAM

The TTALL package has been designed to be run by a part-time program co-ordinator and selected community resource people. The program is based on a model of learning that is interactive. As such, each session contains a number of important elements. The program seeks to involve parents in a variety of learning activities, each designed to encourage them to reflect upon their experiences and role as a parent.

The teaching/learning process followed in the program is consistent with the interactive learning approach described in Chapter 2. Each session of the program attempts to involve parents as active learners and participants.

The program actively involves the parents as much as possible throughout each session. It contains a mixture of short lectures, workshops, demonstrations and apprentice teaching sessions. A critical part of the training is the use of demonstrations of all strategies. These were either held in the classrooms, demonstrated using video footage (which is part of the package) or by the program co-ordinator. As outlined in Chapter 2, these components are in effect presented in a cycle, with movement back and forth from component to component (see p. 19).

The basic components of each of the sessions include the following.

Story reading
The participants are involved in listening to and sharing children's literature.

Leader input
The co-ordinator introduces and discusses a range of issues and strategies concerning literacy and learning.

Demonstration
Opportunities are provided to observe children working in the classroom on strategies which have been introduced.

Discussion and reflection
In every session participants are given the opportunity to discuss the content of sessions and reflect upon their insights and learning.

Homework
Parents are required to put into practice ideas from the program at home.

PROGRAM CONTENTS

The package was designed to provide detailed guidance for the easy conduct of the program. The program consists of 16 two-hour sessions to be spread over an 8-week period. The content of the TTALL program covers learning, issues concerning the nature of reading and writing, basic strategies for assisting children with reading and writing, research strategies, and advice on the acquisition of literacy resources.

The content is organised in seven main topic areas as outlined below.

	Topic	Aims	Content
1	Learning	The aim of this topic is to give the participants an understanding of the important role of the parent as their child's first teacher and to assist them to be aware of the importance of the development of high self-esteem in their children to encourage learning.	• Explores the basic conditions in which children learn • Explores the factors influencing the development of a child's self-esteem • Highlights the importance of a child's self-esteem and its effect on learning • Provides an opportunity to share a number of pieces of literature
2	The Reading Process	These sessions aim to provide knowledge of how children learn to read.	• Gives the participants an understanding of the nature of the reading process • Explores the instructional approaches of reading which help students to construct meaning as they read • Examines the ways in which readers use three major sources of information — semantic, syntactic and grapho-phonic • Introduces strategies for listening to and observing children as they read
3	Supporting the Reader	This topic is designed to stress the importance of providing a stimulating literacy environment at home. 　　It also introduces participants to simple strategies which will assist the child's development as a reader.	• Draws together understandings about early literacy learning and the reading process • Introduces a variety of reading experiences to support children's reading development 　– Immersion in environmental print 　– Reading to and with children 　– Reading predictable texts 　– Paired Reading 　– Directed Reading/Thinking Strategy • Examines the ways in which books support children's reading development

continued

	Topic	*Aims*	*Content*
4	Using the Library	This topic outlines the important role of the library in the school and makes parents aware of popular children's authors and illustrators. It demonstrates to parents how they can encourage their children to become interested in the library.	• Introduces the participants to the school library including the catalogue, fiction and non-fiction sections, reference and resource material • Discusses popular children's authors and encourages participants to experience the delights of reading children's literature for themselves
5	The Writing Process	The aim of these sessions is to increase understanding of how children learn to write. It also makes parents aware that although we write for a variety of purposes, writing has one major purpose, to compose meaning, usually for others to read.	• Explores children's writing development • Studies some common writing behaviour • Examines the nature of the writing process • Introduces the handwriting style most commonly used in the school
6	Supporting the Writer	The first session in this topic aims to introduce activities which will enable participants to support and encourage writing in the home. Subsequent sessions give participants an understanding of the features of quality writing and introduce strategies to parents for conducting a conference.	• Introduces experiences which can encourage children's writing • Provides information concerning the development of children's writing by observing children's writing behaviour and analysing their written piece • Explains the relationship between writing, reading and spelling • Explores the parent's role in helping children become spellers by – Encouraging writing and risk taking – Sharpening children's awareness of words as they read – Developing proof reading techniques

continued

	Topic	Aims	Content
7	Research Writing	These sessions aim to increase participants' understanding of the research process through involvement in the practical activities associated with preparing a project.	• Participants are introduced to a variety of experiences which can assist children to research a topic: – Selection of a topic – Preparing a discovery draft – Categorising information – Note-taking – Report writing • Parents, with their children, are provided with an opportunity to prepare a research topic • Give participants an understanding of skills needed to locate information

TTALL PROGRAM PACKAGE

The TTALL program is outlined in a 450-page resource folder that has a number of key components. The first section of the package contains essential background information including details on setting up the program, publicising the initiative, and its aims.

The second section of the program package is organised into the sixteen sessions related to the seven topic areas outlined above. Each topic commences with a statement of objectives and a list of references and background reading. This is then followed by one to three sessions (depending on the topic), each of which consists of a resource planning summary, a session overview and then detailed session notes for the program co-ordinator.

The program package also includes a variety of useful appendices (e.g. literature lists, graduation certificates, sample advertising, leaflets), a comprehensive parent handbook, overhead transparency masters, a video and photographic resources.

STAGES 2 AND 3 OF THE TTALL PROGRAM

While the above is the major component of the TTALL program there are two additional phases to the complete package.

While the first stage of the TTALL program is designed to equip parents to

RESOURCE PLANNING SUMMARY

ACTIVITY	RESOURCES/EQUIPMENT
Equipment required for most sessions:	STANDARD EQUIPMENT AND MATERIALS

- Television
- Video Player
- Overhead projector
- OHT Pens
- OHT Blank

- TTALL Video
- Textas
- Parent handbook
- Spare pens

1. INTRODUCTION

- Review of Hometask Activity.
- Favourite Books.
- Home Reading Diary.
- Chart with following headings.

Author	Book Title	Recommended by	Approx Age Group

2. WHY DO WE READ?

Parent Handbook, *Why Do We Read?*
OHT RP:1 *Why Do We Read?*

3. STORY READING

Recommended text: Big Book,
Paper Bag Princess by Robert Munsch.

4. READING FOR MEANING

Parent Handbook, *Atwell's Questions.*
See Appendix 6, *Responses to Atwell's Questions.*
Parent Handbook: *Reading for Meaning.*
OHT RP:2 *Reading for Meaning.*
OHT RP:3 *The Mysteries on a Page.*

5. CUES FOR READING

OHT RP:4 *Letters, Words, Sentences.*
OHT RP:5 *Po Kare Kare Ana.*
OHT RP:6 *Reading Diagram.*
OHT RP:7 *Passage without vowels.*

6. OBSERVING THE ORAL READER

Video: Segment: *Listening to your Child Read.*
Parent Handbook: *Listening to your Child Read.*
Pause, Prompt, Praise. Listening to Reading.
Observation Checklist.

7. HOMETASKS

Parent Handbook: *Hometask.*

8. STORY READING

Appendix 4, *Literature Overview.*

T.T.A.LL Programme   **The Reading Process - Session 1**

SESSION OVERVIEW

1. INTRODUCTION
- **Review Hometask Activity**
  10 minutes

2. WHY DO WE READ?
Reading Activity.
OHT RP:1 *Why Do We Read?*
Key Statement: *We read for many different reasons, however our reading has one major purpose and that is to construct meaning.*
15 minutes

4. READING FOR MEANING
Small group activity and discussion
OHT RP:2 *Reading for Meaning.*
Key Statement: *In order for readers to understand the full meaning of a text they must:*
- *Use prior knowledge from previous reading experiences.*
- *Use knowledge of language and the world.*
Key Statement: *Reading is for meaning. Effective readers use a combination of strategies to construct the meaning of a text.*
OHT RP:3 *The Mysteries on a Page.*
20 minutes

3. STORY READING:
Paper Bag Princess by Robert Munsch.
The focus of the discussion of this text will stress that reading is a constructive process.
Key Statement: *'We analyse, criticise, assess, interpret, compare and link books with our own knowledge and experience and generally get inside written language.'*
Atwell.
20 minutes

5. CUES FOR READING
Group activities and discussion which illustrate the constructive process of reading.
Key Statement: *The reader used many cues to make meaning. Letters and words are important but visual cues are not the only cues. Readers also use their own background knowledge and their understanding of how language works to make meaning.*
Refer to OHTs RP:4 *Letters, Words, Sentences,* RP:5 *Po Kare Kare Ana,* RP:6 *Reading Diagram* and RP:7 *Passage without vowels.*
20 minutes

6. OBSERVING THE ORAL READER
Video Segment: *Listening to Your Child Read.* Group discussion and observation.
20 minutes

7. HOMETASKS
Explanation of tasks
- Observe your child reading.
- Listen to your child read and use the appropriate prompts.
5 minutes

8. STORY READING
Conclude the sessions with a piece of literature.
See Appendix 4, *Literature Overview.*
10 minutes

Outline of topics for Stage 2 TTALL Program

TOPIC	AIM	CONTENT
Questioning	This topic aims to make participants more aware of questioning; to consider the use of questioning as a means to discuss text and to explore the four broad categories of questions.	This topic gives participants strategies to use when working with children in the classroom. These strategies include: • Using balanced questioning • Questioning techniques 　　literal; interpretative; 　　critical; creative
The Reading Process	In this topic participants review the reading processes introduced in Stage 1. It aims to create an awareness of the fact that reading is a constructive meaning based act which requires both text based and reader based processes.	Participants respond and analyse a number of texts which illustrate that reading above all is a process of meaning construction.
Children with Reading Difficulties	This topic aims to provide participants with a brief outline of some of the most common problems children experience with reading within the areas of syntax, semantics and grapho-phonic strategies.	Participants are introduced to a variety of strategies which may assist a child having difficulties with reading. These include: Paired Reading and Directed Reading Thinking Activities. Suitable literature for children experiencing difficulties is also presented and discussed.
Writing and Conferencing	This topic aims to review the process children experience as they write, and explores the participant's role in supporting children's writing	Participants are provided with the opportunity to revise editing procedures introduced in Stage 1 and discuss the participants role in conferencing writing. Opportunity is provided for participants to conference with 2/3 children.

work with their own children, Stages 2 and 3 seek to develop school and community resource people.

Stage 2 of the program consists of 8 two-hour sessions that are based around classroom work with children other than the parent's own. Through a range of practical experiences and periods of observation parents are equipped to act as school resource people.

Stage 3 of the program involves a further 5–6 week program designed to provide parents with the skills necessary to share the insights they have gained with other parents. This part of the program is developed around a series of

How's the Kit Organised?

The Community Tutors Kit is divided into eight modules and caters for children from Preschool to Year 6. The package has eight separate modules which can be used in different combinations depending on the age of the children.

Modules Available	Preschool and Kindergarten	Kindergarten to Year 2	Year 2 to Year 4	Year 4 to Year 6
1. Supporting the Reader & Writer	✓	✓	✓	✓
2. Reading together	✓	✓		
3. Reading at home		✓	✓	✓
4. Books to Share	✓	✓	✓	✓
5. Paired Reading			✓	✓
6. Writing together		✓	✓	✓
7. Projects			✓	✓
8. Learning through Play	✓	✓		

one-hour packages which parents subsequently use with other parents in their homes. The total program consists of eight modules and caters for children from pre-school to grade 6. The modules are used in different combinations depending on the age of the children. This part of the project has the added advantage that parents work with parents.

A further extension to the program is now in preparation. It is called *Effective Partners in Secondary Literacy Learning* (EPISILL) and has been funded by the Disadvantaged Schools Program following the initiative of a group of parents in Western Sydney. This program for secondary school parents will be available in 1993.

EVALUATION OF THE TTALL PROGRAM

The TTALL program has been evaluated fully using a variety of qualitative and quantitative measures. A number of interesting findings have been obtained. The data on which these findings have been based included the following:

- pre- and post-test information for all students whose parents are involved in the project — comprehension, vocabulary, spelling, attitudes to reading and writing.
- interviews with all parents before and after the program (these varied in format but included small group structured interviews, large group unstructured interviews, and individual interviews);
- videotaping of parents at various stages throughout the project;
- field note data (recorded by Program Co-ordinator and Assistant Principal);
- reflective journal material kept by co-ordinator;
- group interviews with students and school staff.

The full results of the evaluation have been described elsewhere (Cairney & Munsie, 1992a, 1992b). The major findings were as follows.

THE PROGRAM HAS HAD AN IMPACT UPON THE WAY PARENTS INTERACT WITH THEIR CHILDREN

Analyses of parent interviews, and the post-program survey, suggest that the program has led to changes in the way parents talk to and with their children. It appears that parents are:

- offering more positive feedback;
- providing a different focus when listening to children reading (e.g. less emphasis on phonics);

- asking better questions;
- providing qualitatively better responses to their children's writing and reading.

THE PROGRAM HAS OFFERED PARENTS STRATEGIES THEY DID NOT HAVE BEFORE

It is also apparent that the program has provided parents with new strategies for talking to their children about reading and writing. It has also had an effect upon the way parents assist their children. As the following entry from the program co-ordinator's journal shows, the program strategies are being used at home:

> Before class today Tracey shared how she has been using the research strategy at home. She explained that her son in year 10 was required to complete a major project as part of his School Certificate requirements. He was completing a project on Ice Hockey. He had announced on Sunday that it was due on the following Tuesday. Tracey then related how she used the strategy.
>
> *We went through the steps just like you said, you know discovery draft, then we group the information and everything. I showed him how to use the table of contents and the index. He thought it was great, really easy. We grouped the information under the headings. It worked well. I didn't have to do all the work. I thought this session [the research session] was the best.*

Parents in the TTALL program became more aware of the diversity of resources available in the school and community. They became more capable of finding appropriate resources within the community library, were more capable of helping children with book selection and were able to use a range of research skills that previously were not available to them.

THE PARENTS HAVE GAINED NEW KNOWLEDGE

When the post-program evaluation was completed by parents it became clear that they firmly believed they had gained new knowledge. The parents' self-reporting of this perceived growth in knowledge was also supported by observations of them when working with their own children, as well as by their enthusiastic involvement in the program sessions.

The following segment from the transcript of a group session shows how one parent was able to reflect on her own child's progress. She offered the following response when the group was asked by the program co-ordinator whether the course had given them new confidence.

I was saying to Sue today earlier that I've noticed with Stephen he is best left by himself, he will get on and write, I mean he wrote all of this by himself, umm while I was getting tea. Now the only word I had to help him with was 'hatched', he asked for that, but the rest he just sat down and wrote. But while we've been here this morning, I had to write the first sentence (he asked me) so he could think of the story, and he just fiddled and looked around the room, watched the other kids. I, I do find that he likes to be left on his own to just get on and do it.

THEIR FAMILIES HAVE BEEN AFFECTED POSITIVELY

One of the interesting outcomes of the TTALL program has been that it is not only the parents and their children who have been affected. There appears also to have been an effect on families generally. This has been most evident in the way they spend their time.

Evidence of the impact on families has also been readily apparent in the informal comments of parents as well as in structured interviews. For example, during an interview one mother (Narelle) described how the program had helped her to work with her elder daughter, which in turn had influenced their relationship.

I have found this activity really great. It's brought my daughter and I closer together. The other smart one just thought he was so clever, but my daughter and I have been working really hard. She really enjoys doing the project this way.

When discussing the Anthony Browne books she was reading with her son, one mother (Marguerite) commented:

Andrew enjoys the books and likes to read them but he doesn't get all the humour. My husband I were reading them together. We just killed ourselves laughing over some of the stories. You know adults can enjoy kids' books in a different way to children. I didn't realise that children's books can be such fun. Some of the little books they bring home aren't interesting but now I know they are to help them to read. The real kids' books are so good.

THESE PARENTS HAVE ALREADY BEGUN TO SHARE THEIR INSIGHTS OUTSIDE THE FAMILY

One quite unexpected outcome of the project has been that it has had an impact on other family members, neighbours, and friends from other schools. For example, the following journal entry details one of many comments made during the program which show that the program is having an impact beyond the parents involved.

My sister's friends' kids can't read. My sister was telling them about the course I was doing. Anyway, they've asked me to help them out. I'm going to show this friend what to do. I'm really excited about it. I feel as if I can really do it now. I showed this friend all the books. She wants to do the course too, but I explained it was just for parents at this school. Anyway, we are making a bit of time for me to go over.

PARENTS HAVE GAINED A GREATER UNDERSTANDING OF SCHOOLS

One of the unexpected benefits of the program has been an increased understanding of the ways schools operate. When asked in the post-program evaluation if the TTALL program had helped them to understand how schools worked, a majority (88 per cent) responded positively.

This common response was confirmed by observations of the parents working in classrooms by the program co-ordinator, classroom teachers and the school principal.

PARENTS HAVE GROWN IN CONFIDENCE AND SELF-ESTEEM

One of the interesting secondary benefits of the TTALL program has been that all parents have grown in confidence and self-esteem. The earlier reported observation that parents have shared knowledge of the program with people outside the school is evidence of this growing confidence. Parents valued highly the sense of achievement in completing the program. At the final graduation ceremony at which certificates of completion are presented, families showed just how important this achievement was for them.

This increased confidence and self-esteem has also shown itself in other ways. For example, some parents have experienced new found confidence in themselves as learners and literacy users. The following journal entry shows how this has occurred for one parent. Before one of the sessions Barbara shared how she had enjoyed the visit to the community library (part of the program). She then offered the following comments concerning her own literacy.

I went to TAFE [Technical College] to improve my literacy but all they did was make you work on bits of paper. I still read word by word you know. My husband said I should read Wilbur Smith but they're too long and I forget what it's all about. I found Wilbur Smith on tape at the library so I have been reading the book along with the tape. It's really great. I'm enjoying reading his stories.

Parent responses to the post-program evaluation also indicate that they feel more confident. Most feel more confident working with their own children (96 per cent) and when working as a parent in the school (92 per cent).

Another interesting finding is that most of the parents in the program (92 per cent) wished to pursue further education. Some of these parents expressed a desire to complete their Higher School Certificate examinations, others wanted to enter the University of Western Sydney's community access program (Unistart), and others indicated an interest in teaching degrees as mature-age students. In fact one parent is now enrolled in the Bachelor of Teaching (Primary) degree.

STUDENTS HAVE MADE SIGNIFICANT GAINS IN READING AND WRITING

Results of both qualitative and quantitative measures have indicated that the children whose parents have been involved in the TTALL program have made significant gains in comprehension, spelling, vocabulary and attitudes to literacy relative to students whose parents have not been involved.

IMPLEMENTING PARENT PARTICIPATION PROGRAMS

It is clear that TTALL has had an impact on the lives of the parents and children associated with the program. Its success and that of other parent participation programs suggest that there is much to be gained from the involvement of parents as partners in their children's school education.

The impact of such programs on the lives of parents and children is illustrated by the following comment made by one of the TTALL parents:

> It's [TTALL] given me a lot more confidence, you know. He's enjoying it. It's a thousand times better than it was when it started, and I've relaxed, so it's easier. And he's writing, and he didn't before, and it's just, I couldn't be happier.

6

Where do we go from here?

We hope that the preceding chapters have not given the impression that parent partnership in education is easy. Our experience suggests that it is not. There are no simple solutions to the breaking down of artificial barriers between home and school. However, what is clear is that this task must be one of the major priorities of every school. Parent involvement is not an optional extra; it is not peripheral to the main game of schooling.

Parent involvement has been widely acclaimed as an essential part of the solution to educational inequalities between various social groups. The goal of many educators has been to provide educational opportunities for disempowered members of our community. But the intention of this emphasis on parent involvement must not simply be an attempt to retrain parents (Smrekar, 1992). What we are suggesting are fundamental changes in the way schools and parents relate to one another.

There is growing evidence concerning the impact of parent involvement initiatives. Evaluations like that conducted for the TTALL program have consistently shown that parent attitudes towards school, themselves, teachers, and their role as parents are enhanced (Becher, 1986; Cairney & Munsie, 1992b), teachers benefit (Epstein, 1983) and students' achievement and attitudes are enhanced (Cairney & Munsie, 1992b).

While on the surface many of the strategies outlined in previous chapters may seem like parent training strategies, initiatives like TTALL are attempting to do far more. As well as providing practical strategies for parents, they are an attempt to build community networks in which parents and teachers provide mutual support for children's learning.

PRINCIPLES FOR PARENT INVOLVEMENT

This sense of community is important. Indeed, we believe that the success of TTALL has been due as much to the development of community support networks as to the quality of the program. Our suspicion is that any number of programs could be successful if they follow some of the guiding principles that have shaped our work. It is important to recap these principles, which relate closely to the four key variables that we described in Chapter 2: content, process, source and control.

CONTENT

We believe that the content of programs should:
- cover learning, reading and writing;
- provide knowledge and strategies readily applicable to parents and their children;
- be child-centred;
- provide a special focus on the way parents interact with their children as they read and write.

PROCESS

Our work has suggested that the most effective process for parent learning is:
- parent-centred;
- experience-based;
- centred around practical demonstrations of patterns of interaction with children;
- facilitative of parent interaction, sharing and reflection;
- one that allows parents to grow in knowledge of each other;
- spread over a period of at least 3 months;
- supported by home tasks designed to encourage parents to interact with their children as they read and write.

SOURCE

It is our belief that where possible parents should provide the initiative for programs. However, our experience shows that in the first instance schools may need to look for strategies which will lead to parent–school interaction.

This is best achieved by:
- getting to know your parents and community well;
- attempting to ascertain their needs and educational expectations;
- providing a range of initial contact initiatives.

CONTROL

Our experience as educators suggests that all people learn best when they feel some sense of control of their learning. Parents are no exception. In order to achieve this we suggest that all parent programs:
- are developed in consultation with parents;
- should be constantly adapted to suit parent needs;
- should be community-based, not simply school-based.

GETTING STARTED

Armed with the above principles, how can a school (or group of interested parents) begin the process of developing partnerships between parents and school? In the rest of this chapter we will outline what we see as the essential planning steps. It is important to stress that the set of steps is not necessarily pursued in a lock-step fashion. As part of this process you may need to return to previous steps rather than simply moving on. As well, it is important to remember that some schools will need to spend more time on some stages than others. Above all, remember that the whole process will take time!

STEP 1 ESTABLISH COMMUNITY EXPECTATIONS FOR LITERACY

It almost goes without saying that if you are to form partnerships with parents, you must be aware of the definitions of literacy that are held within the community, and the authentic uses to which literacy is put. As well, you need to be aware of parent expectations concerning literacy. What do they expect of the school? What do they see as the school's role in literacy development?

How is this to be achieved? Ideally it will be achieved as parents and teachers work together. However, in the first instance it may require schools to take some initiative to gain a broad understanding of their parent population. The major strategies for doing this are outlined below.

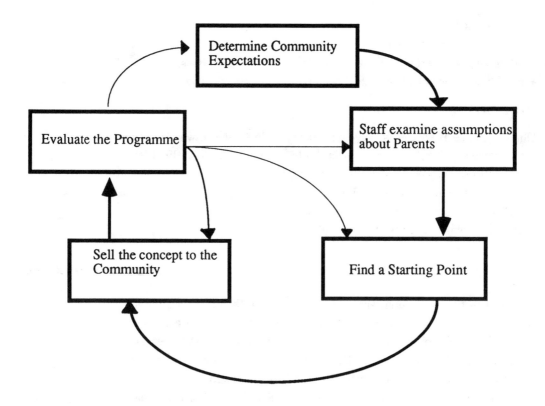

Parent entry interviews

When children are first enrolled at school is an ideal time for the school to ask some basic questions about literacy. The following instructions and questions can be used:

> The school is interested in finding out about your ideas on literacy. We're also keen to know how literacy is used in your home. The answers to these questions are of great help to us when planning to meet your child's literacy needs.
>
> - How often do you see your child reading or playing with books at home?
> - Do you encourage book reading at home? IF YES ASK: How do you do this? IF NO ASK: Are there other things that you spend time doing with your child?
> - How many books (roughly) do you have in your home?
> - Do you read often? IF YES ASK: What type of reading material do you read?
> - Now that your child has started school, what do you see as your role in helping him/her to learn to read and write?

Parent interviews at home

Another useful way to find out more about parental attitudes to literacy learning is to conduct interviews at home. The great advantage of these interviews is that they enable you to meet parents on their territory. Teachers who conduct these interviews indicate that the majority of parents respond positively to this initiative.

It is also possible when visiting homes to find out other useful information about children's family backgrounds. If wanting to try this approach we recommend the following procedure.

- Conduct interviews with another colleague teaching the same grade (if possible).
- Allow the parents to choose a time that suits them (5.00–8.00 pm seems to work well).
- Try to make the interview as informal as possible: in fact, call it a 'chat'.
- If there are two parents at home, try to have both present for the interview.
- Children are an optional extra. Some interviews work best without them, whereas at times the presence of children can relax all parties.
- Send a letter to all parents inviting them to take part. Follow this initial letter with a phone call to confirm details.
- When you visit the homes of your parents use the following procedures.
  - Begin by chatting informally about their children, your programs at school and any other known interest.
  - Indicate the purpose of the interviews once again.
  - Have a note book to write down responses or, alternatively, have an interview schedule with spaces for comments.
  - Ask the following questions.

- Does your child read very often? Has he/she always shown the same level of interest?
- What has been your role in helping him/her to learn to read?
- Do you encourage book reading at home? IF YES, ASK: How do you do this? IF NO ASK: Are there other things that you spend time doing with your child?
- Where do your children get most of their reading material from?
- What type of material do you encourage them to read?
- Do you read often? IF YES, ASK: What type of reading material do you read?
- What do you see as your role in helping them to learn to read and write?
- What would you like school to do for your child?
- What would you like us to do in order to improve your child's literacy?

Sample Letter

Dear ......,

In order to plan the best possible literacy program for your child Ms Blank and I would like to visit you to talk about what you see as the priorities for your child this year.

We believe that parents have a vital part to play in a child's education. As a result we want to ensure that we work closely together.

Could you please complete the attached slip if you are willing to have us visit. We will phone all willing parents at a later stage to confirm the arrangements.

Sincerely,

Ms Blank & Ms Blonk

....

Please complete and return to Ms Blank or Ms Blonk. I/we would/would not like to have a home visit. I/we would prefer the following days and times (please offer several alternatives):

....

....   Phone No. ....

- At the conclusion of the interview thank the parents, tell them a little about your ideas for literacy improvement and suggest that they might like to visit you at school later in the year.
- When you leave make notes of other matters of interest including the number of books evident in the home, and parent attitudes to literacy.

One of the exciting things about the use of parent interviews is that the more interviews you conduct the more open parents become. As well, they begin to offer qualitatively different insights. One of Trevor Cairney's doctoral students (Jenny Power) has been using the interview technique in a collaborative project with a Kindergarten teacher (Anne Rodger). The first interview for the year was held in parents' homes. The second interview was held at school and began with the simple question:

We thought we'd start by asking you to tell us again about -----. Have you noticed any
changes in him since we last spoke during the home visit?

Jenny and Anne have found that after the first interview parents provided detailed observations of their child's literacy progress and attitude to reading and writing. Furthermore, these observations have frequently taught them new things about the children. One parent commented:

She's forever got a pen and paper at home. Her toys don't take a very big part at all.
She's continually writing these different sorts of letters all over the place and she's
asking me how to spell words. Simone comes home and she has homework and
Merissa will sit and look and she's continually picking out double 'o' words, there's
'oo' words. And she's picking out words like 'it' and 'is' and she picked out the start of
'Monday' in Simone's name. So she picked that out. She's reading a lot, she's started
to memorise books from home. She's pointing to the words as she's reading them.

Interviews provide the teacher with valuable insights into the literacy growth and needs of each child. But as well, they provide a basis for building common ground. This is essential if a significant relationship is to develop between the home and school. As this occurs, it becomes easy to nurture and support this growing relationship through direct contact and in written forms (like the letter overleaf).

Written surveys

A further option is to have parents complete a survey. If you choose this option you need to be aware that it is often difficult to get responses to surveys. Reminders will be necessary, and in some cases, no response will be received. This is particularly the case with parents with low levels of literacy. An alternative to overcome this problem is to design the survey as a student assignment, with the children asking their parents the questions provided, and then recording the responses.

The purpose of the survey can vary greatly. The questions asked may include many similar to those outlined above for interviews. Alternatively, the survey might simply act as a starting point for further home/school contact. The example from Lethbridge Park School (overleaf) is typical of the second type.

Lismore   P.S.
10th April, 1992

Dear   Parents,

We wish you all a safe and happy Easter holiday. It is hard to believe that Term 1 of Kindergarten is now over! We are looking forward to a relaxing break to recharge our batteries and ready our-selves for the excitement of Term 2.

Thank you for your interest in our classroom and for the warm welcome we have received in your homes. We have enjoyed learning from you about the "individuals" in our class, in particular about their histories, likes and interests.

Your comments about the children settling happily into school life have been reassuring and encourag-ing. Please keep us informed about their progress at home. We will be in touch next term and look forward to working with you to support your child's   learning.

Kind   regards,

Anne & Jenny

LETHBRIDGE PARK PUBLIC SCHOOL

PARENTS QUESTIONNAIRE

Good schools work closely with their communities. We have a growing body of parents who participate in school activities and feel happy coming to school if they have questions concerning their children's education. We believe that there may be others of you who would like to know more or who have suggestions for us to consider.

Please fill out the following to let us know what you think.

1) I usually know what is going on at school because:

   a) I read the notes
   b) My child tells me
   c) I come to school and ask

2) I understand the sorts of things the children are doing at school because:

   a) I come to grade day
   b) My child tells me
   c) I come to school and ask

3) I would like to know more about what children do in: (Please tick)

   a) Maths
   b) English
   c) Science and Technology
   d) Human Society and its' Environment
   e) Personal Development, Sport and Health
   f) Creative and Practical Arts
   g) Other _____
   h) _____
   i) _____

4) I would like to attend discussion sessions or demonstration lessons on the above. Yes/No

5) I work, but would like to attend evening sessions. Yes/No

6) I would like to attend sessions on behaviour management. Yes/No

7) Any further suggestions you would like us to consider.

NAME: _____ (Optional)

STEP 2 HAVE STAFF EXAMINE ASSUMPTIONS CONCERNING PARENT INVOLVEMENT

A second important step in the development of effective partnerships between the home and school is to have teachers examine their assumptions concerning:

- the role of parents in children's literacy education;
- parent capabilities as supporters of literacy;
- the teacher's responsibility towards parents;
- parent involvement in schools;
- parent attitudes towards school.

How is this to be done? We suggest that at least two staff meetings be set aside for this purpose. The meetings might include the following ideas:

Meeting Idea 1

Provide staff with a short paper or extract from a publication on parent involvement to read. Ask them to come prepared to talk about the paper at a meeting. Break the staff into groups to examine these questions.

- Why would we want to do this?
- How will it affect what we do?
- What benefits would there be?

Meeting Idea 2

Present the staff with the six myths outlined in Chapter 1. Break the staff into groups of 3–5 to discuss each. Bring all staff back together for a combined discussion of their ideas. Provide them with a copy of Chapter 1 of this book. Ask them to come back prepared to discuss it at a future meeting.

Meeting Idea 3

Invite several parents to come to a meeting to discuss the following three issues.

- What do they want for their children?
- What they expect of the school? What type of support do they need?
- What type of feedback would they like?

The parents chosen should have children of different ages and be made aware of the purpose of the meeting. It is important to choose parents who will not simply come along to be negative.

Following this visit have staff consider: how they might find out more about the views of parents; the impact that responding to their comments might have for teachers and the school; the parents' perceptions of their role and their relationship to the school.

Meeting Idea 4

Invite a visiting speaker who has been involved in a parent partnership initiative to come along to share his/her experiences of working with parents.

Examine the six myths about parents outlined in Chapter 1 to consider how they match the experiences of this person.

STEP 3   FIND A STARTING POINT

Once staff have begun to consider seriously their assumptions concerning parents, and their responsibilities towards them, you are ready to consider starting points for parent initiatives.

At this stage the starting point may be obvious because of your initial exploration of community expectations. Your interviews with parents or surveys may have shown that quite specific needs are apparent. If not, you will need to spend more time considering the options. You might also invite teachers and parents from other schools who have been involved in parent partnership programs.

Irrespective of the stage you are at with the identification of a starting point it is important to evaluate what you are currently doing. A good way to do this is by using the table in Chapter 2 (p. 21) that outlines the various types of home/school initiatives.

Use this table both to assess the things you have done, and the content and processes you believe you now need to use. It is important to stress that there is no right way to begin. Some schools may provide virtually no written information for parents. If so you may need to start by providing basic written communication with parents. In other cases, this may be in place, but it may have deficiencies that need to be corrected. In other schools it may be obvious that parents need far more knowledge of what goes on in schools. If so, a series of workshops might be planned. On the other hand, your school might be ready for a support program like TTALL.

When making decisions about a starting point it is important to involve all staff and to seek parent response to the initiatives. It is our belief that the best initiatives are those that have the support of both the school and parents. In the initial stages widespread community support might not be possible, but ultimately this needs to be your aim.

STEP 4 SELL THE CONCEPT TO THE COMMUNITY

Once you have decided on your starting point you need to promote the initiative. The major purposes of publicity and promotion are to tell and convince would-be participants about the program, as well as convincing them of the benefits and keeping them involved in it.

The parent program can only succeed if it has the support of the staff and key community members. Parents have to be continually presented with an array of information before and during the program. One-shot publicity campaigns are usually ineffective because there is no follow-up to build and sustain an initial interest (Farlow, 1982). The following ideas will help with promotion.

Make contact

Make contact with as many parts as possible of the school community in the promotional campaign. Generating a broad base of support is important to the success of the program, and publicity that reaches as many different groups as possible can make them feel they are part of the program (Fredericks & Taylor, 1985).

Name that program

This step is mainly applicable for workshop and support programs. In order to fix a program in people's minds, it is helpful to have a catchy phrase, title, acronym or symbol that is easy to remember. Displaying and promoting these attention getters makes the program familiar and creates an interest. Psychologically, people need to hear or see a slogan or symbol many times before an association with it becomes automatic and can be acted upon.

Getting the message across

Whatever the promotional effort, it is important to convey one important message to parents: their involvement will ultimately benefit their children. Parents must believe that their participation in the program will lead to improved attitudes to reading and writing and increases in achievement in the literacy development of their children. The campaign should also emphasise the role that the entire family plays in a child's academic growth, especially reading and writing skills (Fredericks & Taylor, 1985).

Confidence in the program

Parents must be made to feel they are participating in a program which will be fun, important to their children's schooling and non-threatening. People are drawn to popular activities, so if parents are excited about and involved in the program the others will want to be involved too.

PRODUCING PUBLICITY MATERIAL

With these basic steps in mind it is then necessary to begin producing quality publicity material. The following should be considered.

1 The ideas and facts should be stated briefly, and pitched to the interest of the audience.

2 The language should be very specific and able to be clearly understood. That is, it must be free of jargon. Rarely will parents spend much time on written messages that are not simple, direct and specific.

3 Children should be involved in designing, illustrating and especially distributing some of the promotional materials to parents. Doing so provides children with a meaningful learning activity as well as building up the students' anticipation of the program and involvement in it. Parents sometimes pay more attention to something their child has helped create than to letters from school.

4 Letters can be effective if distributed effectively. It may be worthwhile mailing some directly to homes. This also increases impact. See examples on pp. 82–3.

5 Most local community newspapers are supportive of schools. Use them! Ideas include:

- Letters to the editor. A well constructed positive letter can be a powerful means for informing the public about the beginning of the program and about how parents can contribute to its success and growth (Fredericks & Taylor, 1985).

- Community or educational news section. This section offers an excellent opportunity to discuss parent involvement and the specific value of the parent program (see p. 84).

- As with the TTALL program, the logo or symbol will be easily recognised by the parents. Special insertions in report cards is one way of getting immediate attention from parents, too.

6 Local radio stations often have public service announcements about forthcoming projects. This 20–30 second time segment offers an excellent and cost-effective way to promote the program.

7 One of the most effective methods of selling is personal contact with the parents. In fact, word of mouth is probably as effective as any promotional

APPENDIX 2.1
INVITATION TO PARENTS

Talk To a Literacy Learner

T.T.A.L.L. Program

How Can Parents Help Children to Read and Write?

The TTALL Programme gives you the ANSWER.

As the name of this Programme suggests, TALK TO A LITERACY LEARNER helps parents to talk to and help their children with reading and writing.

> I'm glad I did this Programme. It has given me more confidence to help my children with all aspects of their learning. Anne

> I wish I'd known about this Programme when my older children were growing up. They have really missed out. Maria

> Grant has improved 100% to what he was last year. I think its only that I've relaxed and not kept on at him. Deborah

Come along to our TTALL Meeting on _____ and hear more about the Programme.

Morning Tea is provided

— —

I am very interested in learning more about the Talk To A Literacy Learner Programme.

Name: _____

Child's Name: _____

Class: _____   Telephone No: _____

Return slip to the TTALL Co-ordinator by _____

209

APPENDIX 2.2
PARENTS RESPONSE LETTER

Talk To a Literacy Learner
T.T.A.L.L. Program

INVITATION TO ALL PARENTS

Dear Parents,

The *Talk To A Literacy Learner* programme (TTALL) will be organised for parents at our school. This Programme has been developed to help parents work with their children as they read and write. Parents who join these sessions will become very involved in their child's literacy development.

WHAT'S IT ALL ABOUT? ....

The TTALL program aims to help parents understand better their child's literacy development. Sessions provide practical ideas for parents to encourage their children at home with reading and writing. Opportunity is given to parents to observe and work with their own children in the classroom during some of the sessions.

WHO'S IT FOR?

Parents who have children attending this school and/or pre-school are most welcome to attend.

WHAT DO I HAVE TO DO?

The course will run for eight weeks, two days per week, for two hours per day. Parents will be asked to work with their child at home on a variety of practical activities which will encourage the literacy development of their child.

WHEN DOES IT START?

Introduction to the programme will be held on _____
at _____ in the _____

If you would like to participate in the TTALL Programme, please complete the form and return it to school. For further information, contact the TTALL Co-ordinator.

Hope to meet you at the introductory meeting of the Talk To A Literacy Learner Programme.

_____
TTALL Co-ordinator

210

Standing TALL against literacy

As the international Year of Literacy draws to a close, the University of Western Sydney, Nepean are conducting a program that will provide new insights concerning the important links between the home and schooling.

Parents from Lethbridge Park Primary and Pre-Schools recently graduated from a literacy project conducted by the UWS Nepean.

The program has been designed to train parents to interact more effectively with their children as they read and write, whilst showing the parents a range of strategies to improve their ability to help their children's literacy.

The project entitled Talk to a Literacy Learner (TALL) is an initiative of UWS Nepean, in conjunction with teachers from Lethbridge Park Primary and Pre-Schools.

According to the project director Dr Trevor Cairney the program has given parents greater confidence and skills when helping their children read and write.

"This is an education program for parents to help them work more effectively with their children," said Mr Cairney.

"They observe the children and work with them, teaching parents how to work with their own children and to provide the right assistance," he added.

The participating parents have been actively involved working with their own children in the classrooms as well as at home. The children are enthusiastic about their parents involvement and appear to be developing a more positive and co-operative attitude to being helped with reading and writing at home.

30 parents graduated from this program last month feeling they can now have a more active role in their childs education, being able to help them learn in a professional manner.

"Many parents wanted to do the program either because their own children had learning difficulties or because they wanted to learn more and do a better job with their children," said Mr Cairney.

The program teaches parents spelling, research techniques, including research in the library, how to read with their child, how to listen and how to respond when they make mistakes.

This involves parents working more closely with their children and homework included doing activities with their children at home.

"The course generated high interest in the community and most parents who graduated this year will work next year in a second stage, where they will help other peoples children and act as voluntary part time teachers." said Mr Carney.

"The first training course will be repeated and the project is aimed to be a regular programme," he added.

This is a pilot programme with evaluations being carried out for the ministry of education. It is expected the program will be implemented throughout Australia.

---

effort. Personal contact, either with the person or over the phone, is very effective in informing people about the implementation of the program and provides a way to invite them to become an active participant (Fredericks & Taylor, 1985).

8   Assemblies, grade meetings, school council and parent group meetings are a valuable way of informing the public about the program.

9   The use of a promotional video at a parent meeting can be valuable in informing members of the school community about the program. Photos and examples of children's work can be displayed to inform and 'sell' the parent program.

Promoting and publicising any parent program must be essential ingredients in the implementation phase of the program. It is important to tell parents and the community about the parent program to enlist their support and involvement.

STEP 5 EVALUATE THE PROJECT

A final and critical part of the home/school program is to constantly evaluate the impact and effectiveness of the initiatives. The following questions might help to focus your evaluation.

- Are parents involved? What is the level of parent involvement?
- Are parents gaining new knowledge about literacy?
- Are parents gaining new knowledge about schooling?
- Are parents gaining increased insight into their own children as literacy learners?
- Are teachers gaining new knowledge about students as readers, writers and learners?
- Are teachers gaining new insights into the needs of the community they serve?
- Are the initiatives having an impact on student attitudes to and achievement in literacy?
- Are home/school barriers being broken down?
- Have parent and teacher attitudes towards each other changed?
- Have there been any other benefits?

To evaluate your initiatives in the light of questions like the above you will need to spend time seeking the views of parents, students and teachers. The procedures to be used are very similar to those for Step 1, that is:

- interviews — home or school, structured or unstructured;
- surveys — open ended, rating scales etc.;
- group discussions with parents, students, teachers or a combination of these.

As well, you might want to consider school-wide assessments of literacy. This might include measures such as the following.

- Library usage data: Have borrowing rates increased? Has the type of reading material borrowed changed?
- Observation of reading and writing: Do students read and write more often (home and school)? Has there been a change in the content of reading and writing?
- Have there been changes in school-wide performance on standardised tests?

- Have there been any significant changes in the performance of students relative to literacy profiles?
- Have student attitudes to reading, writing and school changed?

These are just some of the many options available for evaluating your initiatives. It is important to stress that this is an ongoing process. It should be our task to constantly monitor the various strategies that we are using. Without this there can be little assurance that we are achieving our purposes.

Conclusion

We have attempted in this book to give you a sense of the possibilities that are available for parent involvement. We are excited about the many attempts that are being made by schools, preschools and community groups around the world to involve parents as partners in education. We recognise that there is a long way to go, but we are encouraged by the success of many of these initiatives.

As we have outlined in earlier chapters, there are many ways to build partnerships with parents, but so often our initiatives do not go far enough. It is a truism to say that parents have a vital role to play in their children's literacy education. However, we need to constantly remind ourselves of this fact so that we will strive for more meaningful relationships with our communities.

Parent initiatives provide considerable promise, and yet at the same time they have the potential to contribute inadvertently to the mismatches between the literacy practices of home and school, by emphasising a limited range of literacy practices. The latter will be the case if schools continue to view parent involvement as simply an opportunity to have parents 'help' in the classroom, or a means to 'improve' their parenting skills. There are many challenges for teachers, one of the most obvious is the need to build more effective partnerships with families and communities.

As the title of our book suggests, we believe that far too often our efforts to work with parents have tended to place teachers in the position of power and authority. This in turn has done little to lead to significant parent involvement. The research evidence we cited in Chapters 1 and 4 makes it clear that home factors have a major bearing on children's success in school. This reflects both the different ways in which specific cultures prepare their children for schooling, and the fact that schools implicitly, but unintentionally, privilege specific discourses and literacy practices while failing to acknowledge others. Parent involvement is important not just to allow parents and their children to gain access to a variety of literacy practices, but also to facilitate changes in schools and teachers that will enable them to be more responsive to community needs. This development of 'intersubjectivity' (Vygotsky, 1978) is a vital starting point if inequities in education are to be challenged. For many years teachers and educators have worried over that small proportion of students which has difficulty with literacy in schools, and have sought solutions through different or 'better' methodology. We are less than convinced that this is the solution. Rather, we need to engage in social evolutionary development by providing opportunities and alternative programs and curricula which challenge existing educational practices. The work in parent and family literacy in the past two decades has given us some hope that long term reform of the practices of schooling are possible. These practices will lead hopefully to a greater sense of partnership between schools and their communities, and in time will ensure greater equity in the access that students of varying backgrounds have to the literacy practices of schooling and the 'outside' world. We must strive to move beyond the token involvement or acceptance of parents in schooling. If children are to be given equal opportunity to use literacy for self-empowerment, then this is an imperative. It is only when we move beyond tokenism that parents truly become partners in children's literacy development.

References

Au, K. and A. Kawakami. 1984. Vygotskian Perspectives on Discussion Processes in Small-Group Reading Lessons. In *The Social Context of Instruction,* edited by P. Peterson and L. C. Wilkinson. Portsmouth, NH: Heinemann.

Auerbach, E. 1989. Toward a Social-Contextual Approach to Family Literacy. *Harvard Educational Review* 59: 165–181.

Becher, R. 1986. Parent Involvement: A Review of Research and Principles of Successful Practice. In *Current Topics in Early Childhood Education*, Vol. VI, edited by L. G. Katz. Norwood, NJ: Ablex.

Bourdieu, P. 1977. *Cultural Reproduction and Social Reproduction.* In *Power and Ideology in Education,* edited by J. Karabel and A. H. Halsey. New York: Oxford University Press.

Briggs, F. and G. Potter. 1990. *Teaching Children in the First Three Years of School.* Melbourne, Australia: Longman Cheshire.

Builder, P. 1991. *Exploring Reading, Empowering Readers with Special Needs.* Hawthorn, Victoria: Australian Council for Educational Research.

Cairney, T. H. 1989b. Text Talk: Helping Students to Learn About Language. *English in Australia* 92.

———. 1991. *Other Worlds: The Endless Possibilities of Literature*. Portsmouth, NH: Heinemann.

———. (In press). Family Literacy: Moving Towards New Partnerships in Education. *Australian Journal of Language and Literacy.*

Cairney, T. H. and L. Munsie. 1992a. Talking to Literacy Learners: A Parent Education Project. *Reading* 26 (2): 34–48.

———. 1992b. *Talking to a Literacy Learner Evaluation.* Final report of Project funded by the NSW Ministry of Education and Youth Affairs.

———. 1992c. *Talk to a Literacy Learner.* Sydney: UWS Press.

Cazden, C. 1988. *Classroom Discourse: The Language of Teaching and Learning.* Portsmouth, NH: Heinemann.

Delgado-Gaitan, C. 1991. Involving Parents in Schools: A Process of Empowerment. *American Journal of Education* 100: 20–45.

———. 1992. School Matters in the Mexican-American Home: Socializing Children to Education. *American Educational Research Journal* 29: 495–516.

Department of Education and Science. 1967. *Children and Their Primary Schools: A Report of the Central Advisory Council for Education (England). Vol. I: Report* and *Vol. 2: Research and Surveys (Plowden Report)*. London: HMSO.

Eastman, G. 1988. *Family Involvement in Education*. Wisconsin: Wisconsin Department of Instruction.

Epstein. 1983. *Effects on Parents of Teacher Practices of Parent Involvement*. Report No. 346: 277–294. Baltimore: The John Hopkins University.

Farlow, H. 1982. *Publicizing and Promoting Programs*. New York: McGraw Hill.

Fitzgerald, L. M. and A. Goncu. (In press). Parent Involvement in Urban Early Childhood Education: A Vygotskian Approach. In *Advances in Early Childhood Education and Day Care: A Research Annual*, edited by S. Reifel. Greenwich, CT: JAI Press.

Fredericks, A. D. and D. Taylor. 1985. *Parent Programs in Reading: Guidelines for Success*. Newark, DE: International Reading Associates.

Freire, P. and D. Macedo. 1987. *Literacy: Reading the Word and the World*. Westport, CT: Greenwood.

Gambrell, L., R. Wilson, and W. N. Gantt. 1981. An Analysis of Task Attending Behaviours of Good and Poor Readers. In *Diagnostic and Remedial Reading*, edited by R. M. Wilson. Columbus, OH: Charles E. Merrill.

Gee, J. 1990. *Social Linguistics and Literacies: Ideology in Discourses*. Bristol, PA: Taylor and Francis.

Greenburg, P. 1989. Parents as Partners in Young Children's Development and Education: A New American Fad? Why Does it Matter? *Young Children* 44 (4): 61–74.

Grimmett, S. and M. McCoy. 1980. Effects of Parental Communication on Reading Performance of Third-Grade Children. *The Reading Teacher* 33: 303–308.

Harry, B. 1992. An Ethnographic Study of Cross-Cultural Communication with Puerto Rican-American Families in the Special Education System. *American Educational Research Journal* 29: 471–494.

Hanusheck, E. A. 1981. Throwing Money at Schools. *Journal of Policy Analysis and Management* 1: 19–41.

Heath, S. B. 1983. *Ways with Words: Language, Life, and Work in Communities and Classrooms*. New York: Cambridge University Press.

Jencks, C., M. Smith, H. Acland, et al. 1972. *Inequality: A Reassessment of the Effect of Family and Schooling in America*. New York: Basic Books.

Kruger, T. and L. Mahon. 1990. *Reading Together: Magical or Mystifying*. Paper presented to Australian Reading Association Conference, Canberra, 7–10 July.

Lankshear, C. and M. Lawler. 1989. *Literacy, Schooling and Revolution*. Bristol, PA: Taylor and Francis.

Laureau, A. 1989. *Home Advantage: Social Class and Parental Intervention in Elementary Education*. New York: Falmer Press.

Lindfors, J. W. 1985. Oral Language Learning: Understanding the Development of Language Structure. In *Observing the Language Learner,* edited by A. Jagger and M. T. Smith-Burke. Urbana, IL: International Reading Association.

Mavrogenes, N. A. 1990. *Helping Parents Help Their Children Become Literate*. Young Children 45 (4): 4–9.

Moles, O. C. 1982. Synthesis of Recent Research on Parent Participation in Children's Education. *Educational Leadership* 40: 44–47.

Moll, L. 1988. Some Key Issues in Teaching Latino Students. *Language Arts* 65: 465–472.

Morgan, R. T. T. 1976. "Paired Reading" Tuition: A Preliminary Report on a Technique for Cases of Reading Deficit. *Child Care, Health and Development* 2: 13–28.

Nickse, R. 1993. A Typology of Family and Intergenerational Literacy Programmes; Implications for Evaluation. *Viewpoints* 15: 34–40.

Petit, D. 1980. *Opening Up Schools*. Harmondsworth, UK: Penguin.

Rowe, K. J. 1990. *The Influence of Reading Activity at Home on Students' Attitudes Towards Reading, Classroom Attentiveness and Reading Achievement: An Application of Structural Equation Modelling with Implications for Policy Implementation*. Paper presented at the Australian Reading Association Annual Conference, Canberra, 7–10 July.

Rutter, M., J. Tizzard, and K. Whitmore. 1980. *Education Health and Behaviour*. Melbourne, FL: Krieger Publishing.

Smrekar, C. 1992. *Building Community: The Influence of School Organization on Patterns of Parent Participation*. Paper Presented to Annual Conference of the American Educational Research Association. San Francisco, 21–24 April.

Snow, C. 1983. Literacy and Language: Relationships During the Preschool Years. *Harvard Educational Review* 53 (2): 165–189.

Spiegel, D. L. 1981. *Reading for Pleasure: Guidelines*. Newark, DL: International Reading Association.

Street, B. 1984. *Literacy in Theory and Practice*. Cambridge, UK: Cambridge University Press.

Thompson, F. 1992. Making Homework: Models of Homework and Family Involvement. Paper Presented to Annual Conference of the American Educational Research Association. San Francisco, 21–24 April.

Thompson, W. W. 1985. Environmental Effects on Educational Performance. *The Alberta Journal of Educational Psychology* 31: 11–25.

Tizard, J., W. Schofield, and J. Hewison. 1982. Collaboration Between Teachers and Parents in Assisting Children's Reading. *British Journal of Educational Psychology* 52: 1–15.

Topping, K. and G. McKnight. 1984. Paired Reading—and Parent Power. *Special Education—Forward Trends* 11: 12–15.

Topping, K. and S. Wolfendale (Eds.). 1985. *Parental Involvement in Children's Reading*. Beckenham, UK: Croom Helm.

Turner, R. 1987. *SHARE Project—Doveton Cluster: A Case Study*. Melbourne, Australia: Ministry of Education.

Vygotsky, L. 1978. *Mind and Society: The Development of Higher Mental Processes*. Cambridge, MA: Harvard University Press.

Wells, G. 1983. Language and Learning in the Early Years. *Early Child Development and Care* 11: 69–77.

———. 1986. *The Meaning Makers: Children Learning Language and Using Language to Learn*. Portsmouth, NH: Heinemann.

Index